HOW TO START A FIRE WITH WATER

THE SURVIVAL MINDSET

THE SURVIVAL MINDSET

1 Don't Panic!
2 Think Ahead
3 Rehearse Survival
4 Get Organized
5 Fill Out a Personal Information Form
6 Fill Out a Family Information Form
7 Review and Update
8 Get Basic Supplies
9 Stop and Assess
10 Determine Your Resources
11 Know the Rule of 3s
12 Make a Plan

READING THIS BOOK COULD SAVE YOUR LIFE!

Every year, countless numbers of people find themselves in disastrous situations: they get lost in the wilds, or find themselves caught in a flash flood or slide off the road during a snowstorm. Increasingly, headlines are full of ice-storms, wind storms, polar vortexes, blizzards, floods, forest fires, hurricanes, tornadoes, urban civil disturbances, and power grid blackouts, most of which catch the average individual or family utterly unprepared. Even the best-prepared government agencies can handle only so much, and when faced with millions of victims who are caught in a disaster, official responses can be slow, inefficient, or even non-existent. Most people caught in these situations are woefully unprepared and react with shock and fear.

Why, when the news is full of disaster, does this continue to be the case? Certainly, there's a widespread over-reliance on technology and social media for assistance, leading people to feel that they needn't learn even the most basic skills or keep any type of survival equipment on hand. Despite a documented worldwide trend toward extreme weather, many people refuse to take it seriously. Add to this the myriad types of unexpected events such as power grid failures, and the result is a lot of totally unprepared people stranded in

very precarious situations. In general, modern life, with all its ease and convenience, has left many of us feeling somewhat apathetic about being prepared. We think, "That could never happen to me" or "The authorities will take care of it." And that leads to disaster. Most of the victims of these kinds of situations could have survived had they taken an even slightly proactive approach. That's where this book comes in.

I have been teaching outdoor survival techniques and disaster preparedness classes for more than 30 years. During those years, I've also lived on my own off-grid wilderness retreat, where I've put many of these tips to the test. The most important lesson I've learned, and the first thing I teach my students: survival is about being prepared. Reading this book is a good start. The fact that you picked it up in the first place shows that the thought has at least crossed your mind that you might encounter a situation in which you or your loved ones could be in jeopardy. You understand that there are important things you need to know in order to have the best chance at getting out alive—and you are motivated to gain this information. In the chapters ahead, I'm going to guide you along the path to acquiring the basic knowledge and skills that every person needs to be able to face disaster and come out the other side. I call this developing a **"survival mindset."** That survival mindset is what is going to distinguish you from the victims of disaster.

Let's start with the fundamental concepts that underlie the survival mindset—the key to surviving any situation. Subsequent chapters will deal with specific situations, and give practical, step-by-step advice. But first, the basics—how do you acquire a survival mindset?

> 66
> *Panic causes tunnel vision. Calm acceptance of danger allows us to more easily assess the situation and see the options."*
> —Simon Sinek

1 Don't Panic!

This is the number one tip for very good reason. In my classes, I often refer to panic as "the killer." From basic Psychology 101 courses, most of us know that when confronted with danger, humans typically respond with one of the classic reactions of "flight, fight, or freeze." Your heart rate speeds up as adrenaline is released, your muscles tighten in readiness, your blood pressure increases, and your thoughts race. Though these responses can be life-saving, it's better to calm down. The adrenaline rush of panic all too often leads to poor decision making, with disaster as the result. Lost in the wilds, people typically race around in circles trying to find their way out, escalating exhaustion and injury, while making it difficult for searchers to find them. During natural disasters such as hurricanes, people frequently freeze, becoming immobile with fear, instead of evacuating or seeking safe shelter. Stuck in a car at a railroad crossing, victims have been known to frantically try to back up off the tracks or to use their cell phones to call for help rather than simply abandon the car and run like hell! Even worse, panic can be contagious, spreading rapidly in a wave, and further increasing the number of people in danger. So that is why my number one tip is "Don't panic." But how do we tame our fight-or-flight reactions? Take a deep breath! Your brain won't work without oxygen. Read on to find out how to react calmly, tapping into your survival mindset.

2 Think Ahead

Before you embark on any adventure, ask yourself this important question:

"What could go wrong?"

For example, if you are taking the subway or bus to work, "What will I do if service is canceled?" Perhaps you have a weekend boating day planned. "How will I avoid drowning? What severe weather events could I face?" If you know you will be driving on a remote rural highway in the winter, you'll need to think, "How do I deal with sliding into a ditch? What happens if I have a mechanical breakdown?" Getting into the habit of thinking through the potential hazards is a key behavior for people who survive. Practice this regularly!

Rehearse Survival

3

Preparedness is the key to survival. Studies (and basic common sense) show that planning, rehearsing, and simulating survival scenarios can help us to avoid panic—and instead respond intelligently to adverse situations. Thinking ahead is the first step, but it is planning and practice that transform the knowledge you gain from thinking and reading into actual skills. This book is going to show you how to get prepared; the following chapters review a variety of hazardous situations to help you develop the ability to recognize danger wherever you are and understand how to respond to it appropriately, remaining calm and making life-saving decisions. But actual practice is key—repetition imprints the skills into your brain and body, so that you can act swiftly and confidently even in the midst of chaos. I recommend that you find a way to practice your survival skills by taking classes, attending workshops, and keeping your training up-to-date—it could save your life.

Get Organized

4

The very first step in preparedness is to assemble basic information and supplies. People who attend my workshops often want to jump right into action-oriented skills such as building a shelter in the woods, but disaster often strikes in much less dramatic circumstances. For true disaster planning you have start a little closer to home. When embarking on your survival preparedness and prevention planning, an often overlooked but extremely important element is organization, including some necessary paperwork. It is crucial to have emergency information, contacts, important forms, and checklists prepared well ahead of time.

You should have a basic information sheet for each member of your family, plus an accessible location where you have stored the important details regarding your home, cottage or second home, car, boat, or any other vehicle, and office or business, as well as travel plans. I have included form templates in the appendix of this book (see page xx), and you can also find customizable forms online (see Resources, page xx). To get started, take a look at the forms here, and then assemble your information and paperwork so you can fill out these forms all at once; if you leave them unfinished, you may find that you never come back to them. Once completed, keep a paper copy of each form in a safe place in your home (a fire-proof safe would be a good choice) and off-site as well. Additionally, keep a digital copy stored on your computer and at a cloud storage location.

5 Fill Out a Personal Information Form
(Sample form is on page xx.)

This form contains your name, address, contact information, emergency contacts and their information, and your basic medical information. You need one for every member of your family who lives with you. If you have elderly parents or children who don't live with you, make sure you have copies of their forms on hand as well.

6 Fill Out a Family Emergency Form
(Sample form is on page xx.)

Families with children should be sure to develop an emergency plan in case of a disaster and make sure all family members are familiar with it (see Tip # xx.); contact and locations information for the emergency plan should be part of this form.

7 Review and Update the Forms

All your organization is worthless if you don't review these forms regularly. Update your forms each year on the same date or whenever information changes.

Get Basic Supplies and Equipment

8

As part of your commitment to survival, you will need some basic supplies. The specific supplies you need depend on your particular environment and situation, and I will provide lists in chapters ahead. For now, commit to making your initial list of basic survival supplies and obtaining them immediately.

Stop and Assess

9

Despite all your thinking ahead and planning, disaster cannot always be avoided. So when you unexpectedly find yourself in a dangerous situation, what is your first move? **Stop and assess.** First, admit to your situation—you are in trouble—but do not yet act on it. Don't let adrenaline rush in and push you into poor decision-making. Even as your heart is racing, you need to stop, breathe, and tell yourself to remain calm. Your goal is to make a realistic assessment of your situation. In first aid, this is called a "scene survey." So STOP and think. What has happened? Who is affected? What is the immediate danger? If you are thinking like this, you are exhibiting a survival mindset—you are already on the path to survival.

Determine Your Resources

8

No matter what the survival situation, once you have calmed down and admitted that you are in trouble, your next step is to immediately determine what resources you have to help you survive. You will locate resources that are internal or intrinsic (your own knowledge, such as a familiarity with the local terrain), on your person (your basic emergency kit, if you have thought ahead, or if you haven't, whatever you have brought with you, such as a flashlight or an energy bar), and what you can use that is around you (for example,

> *Imagination is an instrument of survival.*"
> —Rogier van der Heide

an empty bucket you can fill with water or use to bail.) The ability to recognize and improvise with resources on hand can make the difference between life or death. For example, many people lost in the wilderness have claimed that they couldn't start a fire, when the reality was that they had flammable materials on them, if they had only known it. Hand sanitizer, lip balm, and potato chips—all are highly flammable. All around you are resources that can be used.

11 Know the Rule of 3s

One of the first rules you learn in any kind of survival training is "the rule of 3s." This information is key, so memorize it! The rule of 3s states that humans can survive for approximately:

- 3 minutes without oxygen
- 3 hours if with unregulated body temperature (i.e., if you become hypothermic or heat-stroked)
- 3 days without water
- 3 weeks without food

Remember that panic shortens your survival time.

Survival Story

A friend of mine was injured in a head-on car crash with a dump truck on a rural road far from cell service. With no ability to call 911, surrounded by a few panicked bystanders not knowing what to do to stop his severe, life-threatening bleeding, he proceeded to calmly instruct the people on the scene based on his sound first aid knowledge, and they stabilized him until paramedics arrived. He saved his own life!

12 Make a Plan

The best time to make a survival plan is ahead of time. Being able to rehearse and practice your plan under non-stressful conditions, and identify problems or missing components of the plan, is crucial. But when you find yourself in an unanticipated situation, you need to be able to plan on the spot. Being in a survival situation also means constantly adapting your survival plan to the unfolding scenario, and thinking on your feet.

1. Size up your circumstances and figure our your immediate survival need—do you need first aid, evacuation, or shelter?
2. What (or who) is at hand that you can use to help you?
3. Prioritize—what do you need to do first to ensure your survival? What else do you need to do?
4. Act—take the first step.
5. Stay positive. Humans are built for survival. Determination and a positive attitude are less tangible but extremely important qualities that will help you to survive.

> "Survival is not about being fearless. It's about making a decision, getting on and doing it, because I want to see my kids again, or whatever the reason might be."
> —Bear Grylls

We will go into greater detail in each upcoming chapter, but you're already closer to surviving than you were before you read this introduction because now you understand the psychology of survival—and are well on the way to developing your survival mindset.

SURVIVE AN INJURY

SURVIVE AN INJURY

Accidents happen! You never know when you or someone else will require first aid. In the home, on the way to school or work, outdoors, and even on vacation—pretty much anywhere—so it's best to be prepared. Everyone should take a standard first aid and CPR adult/child course plus AED (automated external defibrillator) training. If you're an outdoors enthusiast, you should also take a wilderness first aid course.

This book is a very basic primer, and not intended to provide a full range of first aid information. Please do not rely on the information in these pages as your sole source of first aid teaching. Use it to gain a general sense of what you need to learn, then seek out professional first aid instruction.

In this chapter, you will learn how to treat injuries until professional medical assistance arrives. Practice is necessary, and a first aid training course is the best way to get it. Make sure to have an appropriate first aid kit available at your regular haunts (home, country retreat, vehicle, workplace, in your pack while hiking or camping). Understand how to call for help, and what information you need to provide to first responders and 911. An accurate location address and/or GPS coordinates can assist help in getting to you quickly, and being able to explain what happened, as well as what treatment you have provided, may save lives.

13 Assemble a Basic First Aid Kit

For home, office, and vehicle, you should have a basic first aid kit. Keep one in each place. Make sure everyone knows where it is kept. Use this checklist to assemble the items. What do I mean by "basic?" These items will help you to provide first aid until professional medical help arrives. A basic kit is for use in situations when you can call an emergency number such as 911 (most of North America) or 112 (most of Europe). For a more advanced kit, where medical help is not accessible, e.g., in the wilderness or in case of disaster, see Tip #xx. There are many reasonably priced, good quality, pre-assembled kits available at specialty outdoor retailers, and they come in different sizes for various uses. You can find everything from a small fanny-pack first aid kit meant for use while mountain biking or skiing to a variety of larger kits intended for canoe trips or to keep in an RV. If you want to assemble your own, customized kit, start here:

> *If you feel pain, thank God, it's a sure sign that you are still alive!"*
> —Anonymous

- 1 pair non-latex gloves, size L
- 25 adhesive bandages (assorted sizes)
- 2 small gauze pads
- 2 large gauze dressings
- 2 butterfly bandages or Steri-Strips
- 2 non-stick dressings such as Telfa burn dressings
- 2 triangular bandages
- 2 packets NSAID painkiller (such as ibuprofen*)
- 2 packets acetaminophen
- 1 pair first aid scissors
- 1 pair tweezers
- 1 roll first aid tape
- Cling wrap
- 5 packets antiseptic wipes
- Instant heat and cold packs
- 2 elastic roller bandages such as Ace or Tensor
- 1 emergency splint product such as Quick Splint or SAM Splint
- 2 barrier shields for artificial respiration
- Medical information forms (detailing first aid given, for the medics)
- Pocket first aid booklet
- Personal medications

*Not aspirin; giving aspirin to people under 20 can cause life-threatening complications.

Accident First Aid: Do a Scene Survey

14

Whenever there has been any kind of accident, you will usually find panic and chaos. A systemic approach is needed to keep calm and to calm others. The first step is a scene survey or: carefully and quickly scan the accident area to assess the situation and understand how to approach it. You must first ensure your own safety, then see to others'. As you are approaching the scene, scan for anything that could harm you or the patient(s). Once you have made sure the scene is safe for you to approach, you can assess the condition of the victim(s).

15 Run the Safe Scene Checklist

As you approach the scene, look side-to-side, forward, above, down, and behind, and check to be sure there is "No fire, no wire(s), no gas, no glass." In addition to running the safe scene checklist in your mind, keep in mind such potential complications as oncoming traffic, trees that may fall, stinging insects, dogs or other feral/wild animals, swift water, unstable ice, hostile bystanders, slippery ground, steep terrain, low lighting or very dark areas, bodily fluids such as urine, blood, feces, saliva, and even airborne droplets that you can't see (a cough can pose a serious hazard to you and/or to your patient.) Once you've assessed the situation, you can take proper precautions so that the aid you offer is maximized.

16 Know Where You Are

As part of your scene survey, make sure to understand where you are so that you can share accurate information with emergency services. If you don't know, ask someone, use any GPS equipment you or a bystander has, including a cellphone, to figure it out. Pay attention to details, such as what floor of a building you are on or a visible landmark to share with an emergency services dispatcher. Being able to give your precise location to a dispatcher is essential for getting help to arrive quickly, and can save lives.

17 Locate Additional Help

If there are other people around who can help, put them to use to do such things as direct traffic away from the scene, call 911 or find other assistance, comfort uninjured victims, and assist you in offering first aid.

Have PPE (Personal Protective Equipment) Ready

If you intend to provide first aid personally, make sure you always have non-latex gloves and a barrier shield/mouth protector for mouth-to-mouth artificial respiration on hand. Eye protection is also helpful. If you can, be sure to wash your hands before putting on your gloves. Always put on your gloves before touching a patient.

Look for the Mechanism of Injury

When you are sure it is safe to approach, begin looking for the "mechanism of injury," i.e., what caused the injury to the patient. A car accident, a fall, an animal attack, an electric shock—each requires specific treatment, so you must do your best to understand exactly what has happened.

Do Not Move the Patient

Unless there is imminent danger of further injury to the patient or yourself, do not move the patient.

Know Your ABCs

When you are confronted with a person who needs first aid, your first task is to assess the extent and nature of the injuries. One good way to do this is to use the "ABC" technique. Ask the following questions:

- A: Does the patient have an open airway?
- B: Is the patient breathing?
- C: Does the patient have a pulse?

With this information you can provide appropriate care or to give the emergency responders the information they will need.

18

19

20

21

22 Talk to the Patient

If the patient is conscious, introduce yourself and ask if you can help. If the victim declines your help, offer to stay with him or her until help arrives. Ask what happened so you can choose the appropriate treatment or tell emergency responders.

23 Take Off Jewelry

A simple yet important first step is to remove any rings and jewelry or restrictive clothing items at the site of the injury or near an extremity to help prevent swelling.

24 Avoid Biting or Stinging Insects

When the injury is caused by biting or stinging insects, the first thing to do is get away from the source of the problem! Immediately move to a safe area to avoid more bites or stings.

25 Check Whether Patient is Allergic

Some people have a severe allergy to insect bites or stings. For those who experience these anaphylactic reactions, such bites or stings can be deadly. For this reason, make sure that you ask whether the patient has an allergy or has ever experienced a strong reaction to an insect bite. Allergic people should wear a medical alert bracelet, carry at least 2 emergency adrenaline-administering auto- injecting devices, commonly known as Epi Pens, and make sure that others are aware of and know how to use the devices.

SURVIVAL FACTOID

Even a non-allergic person can have a lethal reaction to multiple stings—the more venom injected, the greater the risk.

26 Know the Signs of Dangerous Allergic Reactions

If the patient shows any of the following signs, get medical help FAST or administer the auto-injector:

- Swelling around face, neck, mouth, eyes
- Wheezing, coughing, difficulty breathing
- Hives or itching rash spreading over body
- Dizziness, fainting, loss of consciousness

Remove and treat a Bee Sting

27

Bees have a hooked stinger that can sting you only once but they leave the venom sac behind, pulsating and continuing to inject venom. You'll want to get that out ASAP! Scrape, pull, or brush from the point of entry of the stinger toward the exit point to remove it. Speed is more important than method.

Once the stinger is removed, wash the area carefully but thoroughly with soap and water, and apply a cold pack (wrap the cold pack in cloth—do not put ice or a cold pack in direct contact with skin) for no more than 10 minutes.

Treat a Wasp, Yellow Jacket, or Hornet Sting

28

Hornets, yellow jackets, and wasps have a smooth stinger and can sting you numerous times, injecting venom each time. They don't leave a stinger behind, so you can treat the bite immediately. Raise the bitten area to reduce swelling, apply a cold pack as for a bee sting.

Treat an Insect Bite

29

Blackflies, horseflies, and certain ants, such as fire ants, can give a painful bite that causes swelling, sometimes bleeding, and itching. Clean the wound and, if needed, apply a bandage. Follow with a cold pack for not more than 10 minutes.

Ease the Pain of a Bite or Sting

30

A painful insect bite may be treated with an over-the-counter hydrocortisone or lidocaine cream. If the pain persists or topical creams are unavailable, taking an NSAID or acetopminophen may help.

31 Stop the Itching of a Bite or Sting

A soothing cream or paste may help; choose an over-the-counter product containing colloidal oatmeal, calamine lotion, or an antihistamine.

32 Clean a Minor Cut

If you can see that the wound is not serious, your first step should be to clean the injured area. Keeping wounds from getting infected takes work. Any cut or puncture can lead to tetanus. Tetanus, also known as lockjaw, is a dangerous infection. Flush the wound with water to clean.

33 Treat an Animal Bite

Animal bites can be very dangerous.

- If the bite barely breaks the skin and there's no danger of rabies, treat it as a minor wound. Wash thoroughly with soap and water, pat dry and apply an antibiotic and a sterile bandage
- If an animal bite punctures or tears the skin, use a clean cloth to apply pressure to stop the bleeding. Get medical assistance ASAP.
- If there is any chance the biting animal was afflicted with rabies (which means any wild animal, and especially a bat; or domestic animal whose vaccination status cannot be confirmed, report this to a doctor and seek rabies treatment immediately
- Scrape, pull, or brush from the point of entry of the stinger toward the exit point to remove it. Speed is more important than method.

34 Watch for Signs of Infection

An infected wound requires immediate medical attention and must be treated with antibiotics. If a wound shows signs of infection, seek professional medical help without delay. Prevention is key (see tips below.) Signs of infection are:

- Increased swelling, pain, and redness
- Red streaks from the wound
- Oozing or pus
- Fever

Keep Your Tetanus Vaccine Up to Date

35

After your first shot, you will need a "booster" shot every 10 years. Check with your doctor. Keep your family members' vaccinations up to date.

Stop the Bleeding

36

If a wound is bleeding more than a minor cut, the first thing to do is try to stop the bleeding. Do this by applying firm, steady pressure directly to the site of the bleeding. Do not apply pressure if there is any kind object in the woundIf the cut is minor, bleeding will slow or stop quickly and you can move on to cleaning the wound.

Use a Clean Cloth or Bandage

37

Ideally, use a sterile cloth or bandage to apply pressure to the wound. If you cannot find a sterile bandage, use any clean cloth, such as a tee-shirt, towel, sock, clean diaper or sanitary pad. Use your hands if nothing else is available.

Clean a Wound Correctly

38

Basic wound cleaning calls for thoroughly irrigating the wound with clean water, ideally at body temperature. If you see large pieces of debris, remove them with tweezers. Then run clean water over the wound until you can see that the area is clean. Remember the principle of cleansing the wound from clean to dirty, meaning that the water should run from the cleanest part of the wound to the dirtiest part, so the wound does not get further contaminated. Change dressings as needed as you work.

39   Pat Dry

Use a dry, sterile dressing to pat the wound dry, starting at the wound base and then moving to the perimeter.

40   Apply Antibiotic Ointment

When the wound is dry, check the patient is not allergic to it, and apply a topical antibiotic ointment. Apply the topical antibiotic ointment to the sterile dressing first, and place it on the wound with the dressing left in place as a contact layer.

41   Cover the Wound

When bleeding has been stopped, the wound has been cleaned, and antibiotic ointment applied, wrap up with a gauze bandage and secure with first aid tape, but be careful not to impede the circulation by wrapping it up too tight.

42   Elevate a Bleeding Wound

If possible, elevate a bleeding wound above the patient's heart. For example, if the head is bleeding and you can raise the patient's head without further damage, lift the head onto a pillow. If the arm is bleeding, ask if the patient can hold the arm so it is above the heart.

43   Keep the Pressure On

If the bleeding is not stopping, you need to keep applying pressure until help arrives.Continue to maintain pressure by binding the wound tightly with a bandage or a piece of clean cloth. Secure with adhesive tape.

44   Do Not Remove the Pad or Bandage

If the wound bleeds through the pressure pad, simply apply another one over it. Do not remove the first cloth or you may aggravate the wound, increasing the bleeding. Continue to apply pressure.

Ask the Patient to Lie Down

45

If the wound is more severe, it is best to have the patient lying down, which may help to slow the bleeding. Cover the patient with a blanket if possible.

Treat a Puncture

46

Puncture wounds can potentially be deadly, since the puncture can sever an artery or pierce a vital organ. Never remove the object, and if possible, apply a donut triangular around the object to stabilize, and seal all around the wound puncture with dressings or gauze to minimize bleeding. Get medical help immediately.

Stop Severe Bleeding

47

If, after going through the steps above, the bleeding still won't stop, you may have to also apply pressure to a pressure point. **This is best done by a medical professional.** A pressure point is a place where you can press an artery against the bone. If professional medical help is not available, while still keeping pressure on the wound site, also press against the artery. For a leg wound, apply pressure to the femoral artery in the groin, where the leg bends at the hip. For an arm, press and hold against the brachial artery, along the inside of the upper arm (see illustration.) To check if bleeding has stopped, release your fingers slowly from the pressure point, but do not release pressure at the bleeding site. If bleeding continues, continue to apply pressure to the artery until the bleeding stops or help arrives. After bleeding stops, do not continue to apply pressure to an artery for longer than 5 minutes.

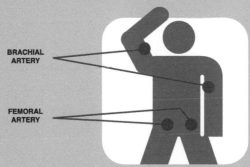

BRACHIAL ARTERY

FEMORAL ARTERY

48 Identify the Degree of a Burn

Burns are treated based on their severity. In order to treat them appropriately, you must first be able to recognize what degree of burn you are looking at.

- 1st-degree burn: affecting only the top layer of skin (the epidermis), this type of burn causes redness, swelling, and some pain. Healing usually takes 3 days to a week.
- 2nd-degree burn: affecting the top and underlying layer (epidermis and dermis), it may turn skin deep red, white, or blotchy; there is also going to be swelling, pain, blisters. Healing may require 3 to 4 weeks.
- 3rd-degree burn: affecting the deeper layers of skin, which may turn white or be charred or blackened, and skin may be numb because nerves have been damaged. Healing may take years.

49 Recognize the Seriousness of a Burn

A 1st-degree burn is considered a minor injury, as is a small 2nd-degree burn. Both of these may be treated by first aid. If a 2nd-degree burn covers more than 2 to 3 inches (5 to 7.5 cm) of skin, or is on the face, hands, feet, face, buttocks, or groin; or if it is over a major joint, it is considered a major burn, and requires professional medical attention immediately.

50 Learn the Source of the Burn

Knowing how the patient received the burn is important, especially when treating majorburns. The most common sources of burns are:

- Sun exposure
- Scalding from a hot liquid or steam
- Contact with fire or flame
- Touching a hot object
- Contact with corrosive chemicals
- Contact with an electrical current

Very hot air, smoke, steam, or chemical fumes can also burn the airways and nasal passages. Be sure to tell any medical personnel how the burn happened.

Wash Your Hands
51

Burned skin can easily become infected. Wash your hands thoroughly with soap and water before touching the patient.

Do Not Ice a Burn
52

Never apply ice to a burn. It can damage already compromised tissues. Always use cool, not icy water.

Cool a First-degree Burn with Water
53

As the least severe type of burn, a 1st-degree burn may be treated with first aid, as can a small 2nd-degree burn. First, remove any jewelry or clothing from the area. Make sure the skin is not broken. For at least 5 but not more than 15 minutes, run cool (not icy) water over the burned area (use bottled water if you are not near a tap), or soak the burned area in a cool-water bath. A clean towel soaked in cool water may also be used.

Leave Small Blisters Be
54

If skin has blistered, but the blisters are smaller than ¼ of an inch (about 1 mm), do not break them. An open blister is more susceptible to infection.

Use Aloe Vera
55

For a minor burn, aloe vera lotion or gel may help. Wait until the skin has cooled, then apply a thin layer over the burned area.

Apply a Bandage
56

A dry, sterile bandage or clean dressing can be applied over the burned area for protection. If the skin remains unbroken, a bandage may not be needed. Be sure to have non-adherent pads and dressings in your first aid kit.

57 Give Pain Medication

If the patient is uncomfortable, ibuprofen or acetaminophen may help. Never give aspirin to anyone under the age of 20.

58 Never Use Butter or Oil on a Burn

Despite what you may have heard, butter, oil, greasy of any type should never be applied to any kind of burn. Instead of cooling the area, oily substances will prevent the skin from cooling, which can worsen the burn.

59 Separate Fingers and Toes

If fingers or toes are burned, they should be separated to prevent the burned skin from sticking. Use sterile, no-stick materials.

60 Treat a 2nd-degree Burn that is not Severe

Soak the burn in cool water for 15 to 30 minutes, using a cool-water bath or clean, water-soaked cloths. When the burn is cool, you may gently pat the area dry, and apply antibiotic cream. Ask the patient's doctor for a recommendation for the antibiotic cream. Apply a clean, non-stick dressing. Repeat this procedure daily, applying the cooling method for 5 minutes, until healing is advanced.

> *Healing is a matter of time, but it is sometimes also a matter of opportunity."*
> —Hippocrates

61 Comfort a Patient with a Serious 2nd-degree Burn

Remove restrictive clothing or jewelry. Call for help or bring victim to get medical assistance. While waiting for medical assistance, attempt to gently cool the burned area with a cloth soaked in cool water.

Put Out Flames: Stop, Drop, and Roll

If a person's clothing, body, or hair is aflame, the steps are:
- Stop: Do not run, flap arms, or make movements that could fan the flames or hinder help
- Drop: Lie down or fall onto the ground, covering the face with the hands
- Roll: Roll around on the ground to put out the flames against the ground.

An emergency responder can assist in extinguishing the flames by dousing the person with water or covering the victim in a thick cloth, like a blanket or coat, to smother flames.

Assist a Victim of a Major Burn

If someone is severely burned, call 911 or take them to a hospital for professional medical assistance immediately. While awaiting medical aid, take the following steps:

- Move the victim away from the source of the burn, if you can do so safely
- Make sure the victim is not in contact with smoldering materials
- Do not attempt to remove burned clothing
- If possible, raise the burned area higher than the heart
- Do not attempt to immerse the victim in cool water
- Monitor pulse and breathing till help arrives
- Keep the non-burned part of the victim covered to help prevent shock

Flush a Chemical Burn

Contact with a corrosive chemical (which may be wet or dry), can cause a burn. Immediately remove the chemical that caused the burn, by wiping it away with a cloth or gloves, or by flushing the area with plenty of water. Be sure to remove clothing or jewelry that is contaminated by the substance. Then check the severity of the burn and take appropriate measures Be sure to tell medical assisters what type of chemical caused the burn. Do not apply antibiotic ointment or any other substance to a chemical burn. Victims of chemical burns should seek professional medical help.

65 Treat an Electrical Burn

Contact with live electrical current can cause a burn. Electrical burns should be seen by a medical professional. To help a person who has sustained an electrical burn, take the following steps:

- Do not touch anyone still in contact with live current
- If possible to do so safely, turn off the power
- Use a piece of wood or other non-conductive material to move the source of electricity away from the victim
- Check the severity of the burn and treat appropriately
- Ensure victim sees a doctor

66 Evaluate a Soft-tissue Injury

An injury to the bodily tissues that does not involve bone is considered a soft-tissue injury, and includes bruises, strains, and sprains:

- A bruise results when force is applied to the soft tissues causing blood vessel(s) close to the surface of the body to break. Any part of the body can be bruised.
- A strain is an injury to a muscle or tendon, such as a pull or tear.
- A sprain is an injury, such as a pull, twist, or tear that affects the ligaments and/or other soft tissues around a joint.

67 Treat a Bruise, Strain, or Sprain with RICE

First aid for a soft-tissue injury is known as RICE (Rest, Ice, Compression, and Elevation), and should be administered ASAP after the injury to most effectively reduce swelling and pain, and help the injury heal faster.

Rest the injured area until it does not hurt to put pressure or weight on it.

- Ice for 20 minutes every hour for the first 24 to 48 hours after the injury.
- Compress by wrapping the injured area to help limit or reduce swelling.
- Elevate the area above the level of the heart to help reduce swelling.

Rest the Injury

68

Surprisingly, people often fail to interpret this instruction correctly. The activity that caused the injury should be stopped immediately, and the injured body part allowed to remain unmoving until it is no longer acutely painful.

Ice an Injury Properly

69

Ice should be applied ASAP. The right way to ice is to wrap a bag of ice or an ice pack in a clean cloth and put it on the injured tissue for 20 minutes. Then remove it and let the skin return to normal. Ice again, as often as is practical, for the first 24 to 48 hours. Never place ice itself or an ice pack directly against the skin. Numbness or redness means "remove the ice."

Improvise an Ice Pack

70

When ice or a pre-made ice pack is not available, any of the following may be used to help reduce swelling until an ice pack is found.

- Use a bag of frozen vegetables or any other frozen item
- Use a very cold bottle of water or other liquid

Apply Compression Correctly

71

A strain or sprain will likely benefit from compression, which reduces swelling and edema (that is, fluid build-up), allowing for better circulation of blood around the injury, which promotes faster healing of the damaged tissues. Use a good quality roller bandage, and wrap all around the injured area. For ankles and wrists, use a figure-8 pattern. Apply firm and even pressure but be sure the bandage is not wrapped so tightly that it restricts circulation. Numbness, tingling, purple or white discoloration or cold skin above or below the compression are all signs that it is too tight. Unwrap and rewrap more loosely. If the bandage causes or increases pain, do not use it. Specialized braces are another option.

72 Elevate a Bruise, Strain, or Sprain

For a lower body sprain or strain, have the patient sit or lie down and prop the injured part on a pillow or other object that lifts it above the heart. For arm and hand injuries, ask the patient to hold the limb up or use a sling.

73 Assume the Worst

If you are far from medical assistance and facing a serious strain, sprain, or possible fracture, assume and treat for the worst-case scenario. You don't have the medical equipment that a doctor or hospital has to evaluate the injury, so always treat for a fracture. The goal is to prevent the injury from getting any worse. If it turns out to be minor, it will heal quickly; if there is a fracture, it will help prevent the injury from worsening while medical assistance is found.

74 Recognize and Stabilize Dislocation

Dislocation is when a bone has been displaced from its normal position at a joint. This usually affects larger joints such as shoulders or elbows, though fingers can also be dislocated. It is usually obvious, and very painful. Dislocation requires medical assistance. Until medical assistance arrives, immobilize the joint using a sling or splint. Untrained people should not try to put dislocated joints back in place.

Immobilize a Dislocated Shoulder

There are two ways to do this:

- Place a rolled up towel or pillow between the person's chest and upper arm. Wrap a piece of fabric or cling wrap around the area to bind the arm to the chest.
- Make a sling for the affected forearm, keeping the elbow bent at a 90-degree angle

Improvise an Arm Sling

If a pre-made sling is not available, make one from a triangular bandage or piece of cloth folded into a triangle.

- Hold the arm across the body. Support the arm above and below the site of the injury.
- Place the widest part of the triangular fabric under the injured arm and place one end over the shoulder on the uninjured side. Bring the other end up to meet it.
- Tie the ends of the sling together at the side of the neck.

Recognize a Fracture

A fracture or break in a bone typically results when force is applied to a bone. This may result from a fall, a blow, an impact, or repeated stress. A fracture can be "open," which means the bone is sticking out through the skin, or "closed," meaning that the broken bone has not penetrated the skin. Suspect a closed fracture if:

- The patient felt a bone break
- The patient heard a snapping sound
- Patient feels a grating

CLOSED FRACTURE   OPEN FRACTURE

sensation upon movement
- The arm or leg is visibly misshapen
- Swelling, bruising, pain or extreme tenderness at the site of injury
- Moving the fingers or toes is impossible or extremely painful
- No pulse at the end of a limb
- Numbness at the end of a limb
- Intense pain upon movement and inability to bear weight

Any kind of fracture requires immediate medical attention.

78 Stabilize a Patient with a Suspected Fracture

Although a fracture is serious, especially if it occurs where medical assistance is not available, an uncomplicated fracture of the arm or leg is not usually life-threatening. First, check for bleeding; apply pressure until it stops. Calm the patient and then immobilize the limb. Apply ice as above.

79 Immobilize the Injury by Splinting

Splinting immobilizes the injured part so movement won't hurt it further. There are two ways to splint an injury so it can't move.

- Attach the injured part to something rigid, such as a rolled-up magazine or a piece of wood—even a hefty stick will do. Anything you can use to tie or fasten, such as tape, cling wrap, rope, a tie, or a belt will work.
- Tape the injured part to some other part of the body. For example, tape a toe or finger to its neighbor or an injured arm to your chest.

80 Splint an Injured Finger or Toe

Simply tape the injured digit to the adjacent finger or toe.

Follow the Joint-to-Joint Rule

81

When applying a splint, the most supportive arrangement is for it go from a joint above the injury to a joint below it. When splinting an injured forearm, for example, choose a splint that extends from above the elbow to below the wrist.

Apply Traction

82

Generally speaking, non-medical professionals should not attempt to move broken limbs back into position. Keep movement of any suspected break to an absolute minimum. However, if you are far from professional medical help, you may have no choice. It is better to have two people do accomplish this.

- Hold the bone above the break (toward the body)
- Gently pull the other end of the broken limb to put the bone back in its correct position
- Apply the splint

Know When Not to Move an Injured Person

83

Never move a person who has a suspected head, facial, neck, or back injury. Call 911 or emergency services immediately. If you can, ensure open airway, breathing, and circulation.

Decide Whether to Move a Patient

84

Evacuate or stay put? For leg, pelvic, and head and spinal injuries, the patient should not be moved until trained personnel get there. However, in life or death situations, e.g., a car is on fire, you move the injured to your best of your ability—and as long as you are also safe. In a scenario of deadly danger, such as a building collapse, shooting, explosion, fire, mudslide, or flood, you may have no option but to drag or carry the victim(s) away from the danger, realizing that you might cause more damage or injury. Move the patient if it's a matter of life over limb.

85 Improvise a Stretcher

An improvised stretcher is used as a last resort, if injuries permit, and if there are enough people to carry the patient out safely. If you must move a patient, an improvised stretcher can be made easily using blankets, tarps, internal framed backpacks, lifejackets, or coats. A jacket stretcher is reasonably easy to make, lightweight, and has sufficient support to transport an injured person. However, it is not rigid, takes some time to construct, and makes the jackets unavailable for rescuers to wear. To do it:

- Find or cut 2 pieces of wood to be poles. They must be 3 feet (1 m) longer than the patient. Poles should be of hardwood so will bend when weighted. DO NOT USE dead wood, as it could break.
- Find 3 jackets, life vests, or anoraks made of non-stretch materials. Do up zippers and buttons.
- Slide one pole through each of the armholes of the jackets.
- Use 3 belts, webbing, or duct tape to reinforce the stretcher approximately where the shoulders, hips and lower legs of the patient will be.

Before carrying an ill or injured person, perform a test lift with an uninjured person. Make sure all shoelaces are tied. Assign one person to do the count. A sample count would be, "Is everyone ready? Lift on 3. 1, 2, 3. Keep it smooth and steady."

86 Keep an Unconscious Person Safe

If a person is unresponsive or very minimally responsive (i.e, moaning but does not open eyes or speak) take the following steps:

- have someone call emergency services
- check patient's airway,

breathing, and pulse
- if patient is not breathing, begin CPR
- if patient is breathing but lying on his or her back, and you do not think there is a spinal injury, carefully roll the person toward you, bending their top leg so both hip and knee are at right angles
- gently tilt their head back to keep the airway open

If breathing or pulse stops at any time, roll the person onto their back and begin CPR.

- stay with the person and keep them warm until medical help arrives

Recognize Hypothermia

87

Hypothermia occurs when body temperature drops below 95°F (35°C); it can become life-threatening quickly, and requires professional medical attention. Severe hypothermia (body temp less than 86°F (30°C), is often fatal. (For tips on avoiding hypothermia, see Chapter 5.) Symptoms of hypothermia:

- intense shivering, numbness, cold, pale, and dry skin
- drowsiness, confusion, apathy or irrational behavior
- slow, shallow breathing
- slow and weakening pulse

Treat Hypothermia

88

Treat by preventing further heat loss and by **slow, gentle warming.** Get the patient indoors, cover with layers of blankets, and give warm liquids (soup is a good choice) and high-energy food. Warm the core first, not extremities. If you can't move indoors:

- insulate patient from the cold ground with a tarp, space blanket, or leafy branches
- remove wet clothes and change into dry ones
- gently put patient into a sleeping bag and cover with blankets, head included

- never put the cold person into a hot bath and do not rub cold limbs.

Overly rapid warming can cause the blood vessels in the arms and legs to open up too quickly, potentially causing a dangerous drop in blood pressure. If you suspect severe hypothermia (shivering has stopped, heart rate has slowed, and patient is losing or has lost consciousness, call for medical help immediately and give CPR while you wait.

89 Know the Signs of Frostbite

Frostbite occurs when the skin and tissue beneath it freeze. Areas most prone to frostbite are fingers and toes, nose, ears, cheeks, and chin. Symptoms include:

- pale or reddened skin that may be waxy and/or hard
- prickling, throbbing, burning and/or numbness

90 Treat Frostbite

Minor frostbite can be treated with first aid measures of slow warming, but severe frostbite, which causes blistering and extreme pain, requires professional medical treatment.

- get out of the cold
- remove wet clothes
- if frostbitten areas may be exposed again and refrozen, don't thaw them. If they're already thawed, wrap them up so that they don't refreeze
- gently rewarm frostbitten areas by soaking hands or feet in warm, not hot, water (99 to 108 F/ 37 to 42 C) for 15 to 30 minutes
- don't rub skin or apply direct heat, as with a heating pad
- do not put frostbitten limbs close to a stove or fireplace
- try not to walk on frostbitten feet or toes

Thawing skin will tingle and burn as it warms up; this is normal. It will usually take from 30 to 40 minutes for skin to be rewarmed and normal sensation and movement restored.

Apply dry, sterile dressings and use them to separate fingers and toes until healed.

Be Alert to Overheating

91

Hot temperatures and/or prolonged sun exposure may lead to heat exhaustion, when the body cannot adequately cool itself. Symptoms:

- extremely heavy sweating
- muscle cramps
- thirst
- fatigue
- dizziness or feeling faint
- nausea and/or vomiting
- dark urine

Treat Heat Exhaustion

92

Untreated heat exhaustion leads to heatstroke (body temperature of 103 degrees F/39.5 C), which can be deadly and requires immediate professional medical attention. An overheated person should.

- seek out a shaded, cool location
- lie down, ideally with feet elevated above head level
- sip cool liquids, ideally a sport rehydration drink or water
- remove clothing and cool skin by fanning, applying cool cloths or water, or cloth-wrapped icepacks (never apply ice packs directly to skin)

Provide Reassurance

93

Though it may not be taught in medical textbooks, reassurance is a powerful healing tool. When giving first aid to any victim, also offer them words of comfort and reassurance that you are here to help, and they are not alone. If you are actually on your own, positive, reassuring thoughts will help--tell yourself, "I can do this. I'm going to be okay."

SURVIVE AT HOME

Chapter 2
SURVIVE AT HOME

*There is nothing
more important
than a good, safe,
secure home."*
—Rosalynn Carter

SURVIVE AT HOME

Most people feel safe at home, and rarely bother being prepared for anything worse than running out of coffee—but accidents frequently happen in and around the home, and disasters can force you out of your home or strand you inside it. Ask yourself: What could happen in our home and neighborhood? You need to take personal responsibility for your own survival (and that of your loved ones.) In North America, during recent hurricanes Katrina, Andrew, and Sandy many local organizations fell apart, and indeed, in some places, civilization as we know it came to a complete stop. Many folks, even those used to having plenty of resources at their disposal, couldn't take care of themselves or their families. Don't be one of those people who is uselessly trying to call out on a cell phone that isn't working to get help; instead, be ready to help yourself and your family. Your survival may depend upon it. As you make your plans, prepare specifically for the most likely types of disasters and do not waste time on the least likely. If you live downtown in a big city, for example, a wildfire is probably not a concern but a major power outage could be extremely problematic. In this chapter, we'll cover tips for everyday home safety, what to do if you need to leave home or "bug out," and how to make your home a safe haven during an emergency.

94 Know How to Call 911

Make sure everyone in your family knows the local emergency number, and how and when to call it. If you have children, elderly people, or differently abled family members living in your home, be sure each of them knows what to do in case of fire, illness, accident, or other emergency. Give examples and rehearse.

- Briefly describe the situation
- Give your location; if you do not know it, ask, look for cues around you, and be as specific as possible
- If you are calling from a cell phone, the dispatcher may

be able to track your location using GPS, so do not hang up

- If you cannot speak, call anyhow and leave the line open, so the dispatcher can try to establish a location and send responders

Know the Locations of Nearest Hospitals

95

Always know the locations of hospital and urgent care centers near your home. Depending on the scope of the emergency, 911 and local ambulance services could be swamped and overwhelmed, and you might have to get to help on your own. Some handheld and vehicle GPS systems have emergency buttons or features, such as "nearest hospital" that includes address, directions, and phone number.

Keep a Landline Telephone

96

In this digital age, almost everyone has a cell phone, and some folks decide that a landline is old-fashioned or a waste of money. However, only a landline will continue to operate if the power is out. Make sure you keep one landline telephone that is directly connected to the phone line. Any phone system that has to be plugged into a power line will not work in a power outage.

Keep Your Cell Phone Charged

97

Your cellular telephone is an excellent emergency communication device. Keep it charged up. Get extra battery-powered chargers, and store at least one extra at every location. Not only is your phone a communication device, it is also a tracking device—most newer phones have GPS capability, which means that authorities can track your location and find you in an emergency—if your phone is on.

Get the Right Cell Phone and Coverage

98

Being able to communicate with the outside world is a

key factor for surviving an emergency. Cell phones can be excellent communication devices, but only if they have coverage. Not all smart phones are created equal, and mobile service providers vary as well. Check to make sure your service provider's coverage areas and communication tower locations are ideal for where you live or travel.

99 Boost Your Signal

A good cell phone booster-amplifier can increase your coverage area and boost your signal in rural and remote areas by as much as 20 to 40 times! Be sure to match your phone with a compatible booster.

100 Post a Home Emergency Information Form

Every home should be equipped with a sheet that lists all local and personal emergency contacts that might needed in case of trouble. List official evacuation centers and your family contacts and meeting places. You should have an emergency information form posted in a prominent place at every property or dwelling that you own or rent. See page xx for an example you can adapt for your own use.

101 Create a Disaster Plan for Your Family

Once you know the types of disasters that could affect your home and family, you will need to create and write down a basic disaster plan for fire, flood, or any other disaster. **A family emergency plan is essential.** Include the following:

- Safe exits from home
- Local and regional meeting places to reunite with family members
- How to leave the neighborhood: evacuation plan
- Designated person to pick up children if parent/guardian is not available
- Local contact person
- Regional contact person
- "Bug out " kit

- Health and insurance information

Write down and rehearse your plan with all members of the family. See the Appendix, (p xx) for a sample family disaster plan. You can find other good examples on-line at www.fema.gov and www.ready.gov in the US and at www. getprepared.gc.ca in Canada.

Practice Your Plan Twice per Year

102

The secret to making your survival plan effective is practice. Make sure you rehearse with your entire household 2 times per year. Any less frequently, and people, especially children, are likely to forget the details. Post the plan in an obvious place for easy referral.

Don't Forget to Plan for Pets

103

If you have pets, you must account for them in your planning. Decide how you will deal with each situation, who will get the pets out of the home, what pet supplies should be taken, and how it is to be done. Make sure everyone knows the plan for pets. For resources to help you plan, visit the Animal Safety section on www.redcross.org or visit the Humane Society Web site at www.hsus.org.

Select a Safe Local Meeting Place

104

Pick a place outside but near your home that every member of your family can find and get to in case of an emergency that affects your home, such as a fire. This could be a local landmark, a neighbor's house (be sure the neighbor knows and is okay with this plan) or a nearby church, store, or school. Make sure everyone knows where it is and how to get there.

Select a Safe Regional Meeting Place

105

If you cannot go home or your neighborhood needs to be evacuated, you must have a safe haven outside your immediate neighborhood that your family members can reach. If the emergency renders your entire city or region a disaster area, family members will need someplace farther away as the emergency meeting place. The home of a friend or relative is ideal; other choices include your second or country home, or RV, an easy-to-find public building, a church, or a community center. Put this information on the emergency wallet cards.

106 Plan Your Exit Routes

Figure out the best ways to leave your neighborhood—on foot, on bicycle, by car or other vehicle, or by public transportation (though it may not be working) and make sure each person in your household knows how to do it. Have an alternate evacuation route ready in case your primary route is blocked. Use a physical map to explain the route to your household members, and keep a copy in an easily accessed location.

107 Select an Emergency Contact Person

In many emergencies, local phone service or cell service does not work. Find an out-of-town family member or friend who is willing to be your family's designated out-of-town emergency contact. Give each member of your family the person's address and phone numbers. During an emergency, instruct everyone to call your contact to find out where family members are and how to get in contact with one another.

108 Add a Secondary Emergency Contact Person

In case your first emergency contact is unavailable, have a second person who is willing to play this role, ideally in a different part of the country than your first person.

109 Check on Your Neighbors

Consider organizing a neighborhood buddy plan to help people in your neighborhood who may need extra help during an emergency, such as elderly or physically challenged people.

Know the Local Emergency Resources

Do you know what to do if a windstorm closes roads in and out from your vacation home or property? Does your RV park have backup power and water sources in case of a lengthy blackout? Does your condo have a contingency plan for a disaster? Do you know the official evacuation route from where you live? Usually, the answer to these questions is a resounding "no!" If you're serious about survival, you must get to know what emergency resources are available to you locally, what your neighborhood's emergency warning signals sound like, where evacuation centers are located, where fallout shelters can be accessed, and where your family members can turn for help. Many urban and rural communities and local governments organize disaster preparedness plans, and have emergency shelters or programs in place in case of earthquakes, hurricanes, flooding, tornadoes, or fire. Find out if such groups and plans exist. If your neighborhood doesn't have any such programs, organize them yourself.

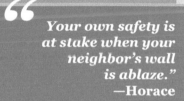

Your own safety is at stake when your neighbor's wall is ablaze."
—Horace

Assemble Vital Personal Documents

Take the time now to organize important documents and put them in a safe place. For extra security, make copies and keep the copies off-site. Use this checklist to help you:

- Picture IDs
- Social security card
- Passports and visas
- Birth certificates
- Adoption and custody papers
- Marriage certificates
- Divorce decrees
- Death certificates

- Citizenship papers
- Bank account information
- Credit cards
- Life insurance policies
- Wills and trusts
- Funeral and burial plans
- Military papers

112 Assemble Important Home/Property Documents

In the confused aftermath of any disaster that affects your home or property, you may not be able to locate any of your important household documents. Avoid this by organizing them in advance and putting them in a safe place, with copies off-site. You will find that having your documentation together is essential in getting post-disaster help.

- Mortgage documents
- Deeds
- Vehicle titles and bills of sale
- Name, address and number of your accountant, attorney, and insurance agents
- Insurance policies
- Important warranties

It is also wise to keep passwords in a separate, written document that you do not store in any computer or device.

113 Make Wallet Emergency Cards

Having assembled all your information, it won't take much extra effort to create a wallet-sized, laminated emergency card for every member of your family. Each card should have the following information:

- Name
- Photo (ideally)
- Description (height, eye color, weight, hair color)
- Age/DoB
- Address

- Phone numbers
- Emergency contacts
- Meeting places
- Medical conditions/allergies/blood type/current medications
- Insurance name and policy/member number
- MDs, dentist

Get Insurance

114

It is wise for your future financial survival to be sure your home and property are fully insured. Consult an expert to be sure you appropriately covered in regard to property replacement, liability, and alternate accommodations, in case of flood, earthquake, hurricane, wind, ice storm, tornado, severe drought, and/or wildfire, plus any other riders and additional coverage relevant to your situation. Renters should have a tenants policy in place, as a landlord's policy will not cover a renter's valuables or relocation expenses.

Commit to a Safe Home

115

Commit to making your home a safe everyday space by installing basic safety devices and ensuring everyone in your household understands how to use them, and what to do in an emergency. Every home needs the following:

- carbon monoxide detector
- smoke alarm
- fire extinguisher
- well-stocked first aid kit
- emergency lighting

Install battery-powered Carbon Monoxide Detectors

116

Remember: wired-in models won't work during a power outage. Install battery-powered carbon monoxide detectors alarms, one on each level of the house or building, including the basement. Locate them near sleeping areas.

Make sure they are in good working condition, and replace batteries annually.

117 Install Battery-powered Smoke Alarms

Install battery-powered smoke alarms, one in each bedroom, and another outside the sleeping areas on each level of the house or building, including the basement. Test them monthly.

118 Replace Battery-powered Alarms Every 10 Years

Home smoke alarms must be replaced every 10 years.

119 Install Fire Extinguishers

You need a fire extinguisher on every level of your home or building. Choose multi-purpose extinguishers, and install one on each floor, near an exit. Make sure you have one in your kitchen. Be sure that everyone in the household knows where the extinguishers are located and how to use them. Check expiry dates and replace as needed. If you have a woodstove or fireplace, you will need a specialized fire extinguisher that can put out a chimney or creosote fire—be sure to obtain one for each fireplace or stove.

120 Create and Rehearse a Home Fire Plan

Any fire in your home can spread fast, leaving you with only minutes to escape safely once the alarm sounds. Survival is much more likely if you have a good fire plan, and you have practiced it. Draw a floor plan of your home, marking two ways out of each room, including windows and doors. Also, mark the location of each smoke alarm. Post your plan where family members see it regularly, and most importantly,

SURVIVAL FACTOID

During recent major hurricanes, tens of thousands of people ignored official warnings to evacuate. The result was a high number of unnecessary and tragic fatalities.

practice. Be sure every member of the family knows what to do if the alarm goes off, and how to get out fast. Online resources in the US include the National Fire Protection Association website, www.nfpa.org (for a downloadable escape planning grid), the Red Cross, www.redcross.org, and the National Safety Council, www.nsc.org. In Canada, visit Fire Prevention Canada at www.fiprecan.ca or the Canada Safety Council, www.canadasafetycouncil.org.

Choose the Safest Escape Route

121

When conducting drills, emphasize the need to choose the route with the least amount of smoke and heat, even if it's not the preferred route that you practiced.

Go Low in Smoke

122

Smoke is toxic. If you have to escape through smoky conditions, the best way is to "go low," that is, crouch or crawl as close to the floor as possible while still moving swiftly. When practicing a fire drill, everyone in the family should practice getting low and going under the smoke to your exit.

Close Doors

123

Closing doors behind you on your way out slows the spread of fire, giving you more time to safely escape.

Conduct a Home Fire Drill Every 6 Months

124

Walk through your escape plan with all household members, checking that doors and windows open easily.

Plan and Practice Upper-story Exits

125

If the home has multiple floors, every family member must be able to escape from the upper-floor rooms. Place safety ladders in or near windows and practice setting up the ladder from a first-floor window to make sure you can do it correctly and quickly. Children should practice only with an adult present, and only from a first-story window. Make sure everyone knows the location of the ladder to avoid having to search for it during a fire.

126 Seal in for Safety

There are times when the smoke or flames can prevent a safe exit from a home or, especially, a multi-floor or high-rise apartment building. To prepare for such a situation, practice "sealing in for safety" as part of your home fire escape plan.

- Close any and all doors between you and the flames.
- Use duct tape or towels to fully seal the door cracks and cover air vents so that smoke cannot seep in.
- If possible, open windows at the top and bottom to let in fresh air.
- Use a face shield over your nose and mouth—there may be one in your first aid kit or you can use a clean, moist cloth.
- Call 911: report your exact location.
- Wave a flashlight or white piece of clothing at the window to alert the firefighters to your location.

127 Prepare for a Flood

If you live in a floodplain your home should be elevated and reinforced by professionals. The furnace, water heater, and electric panel must be elevated. Install "check valves" in sewer traps to prevent floodwater from drain back-ups. Construct barriers (levees, beams, floodwalls) to stop floodwater from entering the building. Seal walls in basements with waterproofing compounds

SURVIVAL FACTOID

It is possible to drown in as little as 3 inches (7.5cm) of water in a period of just minutes.

to avoid seepage. An automatic sump pump or swimming pool pump with hose is helpful to have.

Know the Dangers of Flooding

Flooding can be caused by prolonged or intense rainfall, or when a river or stream overflows and floods the surrounding area. Urban flooding can fill streets with swift- moving rivers of water. Basements and viaducts may be deadly when filled with water. Flash floods can occur without warning within six hours of a rainstorm, after a dam or levee failure, or following a sudden release of water. If you live in an area prone to flash floods, plan now to protect your family and property. Make sure children understand the dangers: **Never play around high water, storm drains, ditches, ravines, or culverts.** It is very easy to be swept away by fast-moving water.

Develop a Flood Plan

If your home is susceptible to flooding, review what to do in the event of a flood with your family. This should be part of your family emergency plan. The rule is: **head for higher ground and stay away from floodwaters.**

- Listen to the radio or television or follow the weather reports online for a flood "watch" or "warning." Be sure to have a NOAA Weather Radio with a tone-alert feature, or a portable, battery-powered radio (or television) for updated emergency information. A watch means flooding is possible; a warning means flooding is imminent and you will need to take action.
- Know if there are nearby streams, dry riverbeds, drainage channels, canyons, or other areas known to flood suddenly. Flash floods can occur in these areas with or without typical warnings like rain clouds or heavy rain. If there is any possibility of a flash flood, move to higher ground right away. Do not wait for instructions to move.

If you must prepare to leave, you should do the following:

- Secure your home. If you have time, bring in outdoor furniture. Move essential items to an upper floor.

- Turn off utilities at the main switches or valves if asked to do so. Disconnect electrical appliances. Do not touch electrical equipment if you are wet or standing in water.

130 **Know How to Turn Off Water, Electricity and Gas**

Make large, easy-to-see signs for water and gas shut-offs in your home, as well as for the electrical panel.

131 **Memorize Flood Safety Rules**

If you encounter moving water or water higher than 6 inches (15 cm):

- STOP, TURN AROUND, AND GO ANOTHER WAY
- GET TO HIGHER GROUND

If you have to evacuate:

- Never walk through moving water. Turn around and find another route. Choose a route with still water if at all possible. Fast-moving water, even water that does not appear to be deep, can knock a person off their feet. This is particularly dangerous for children, older people, and those with physical challenges. Many people are swept away while attempting to wade through floodwaters.

> **SURVIVAL FACTOID**
>
> If you enter swiftly flowing water, you risk drowning, even if you can swim. Swiftly moving shallow water can be deadly, and even shallow standing water can be dangerous for small children. Cars or other vehicles do not provide adequate protection from flood waters. Cars can be swept away or may break down in moving water.

- Keep away from flooded areas. Never walk, swim, drive, or play in floodwater. If you must walk through a flooded area, use a stick to check the firmness of the ground in front of you. Holes and debris are hazards.
- Stay away from creek and stream banks in flooded and recently flooded areas. The soaked banks often

become unstable due to heavy rainfall and can suddenly give way, tossing you into rapidly moving water.

Safely Return Home After a Flood

132

Before you come back to your flooded property, make sure that the authorities have authorized it, and that your home is not condemned, or unsafe to re-enter. You might wish to communicate with your insurance adjuster first, so they can do an evaluation of the safety, and replacement/repairs.

- Return to your home during daylight hours so that you do not have to use any lights. Use battery-powered flashlights and lanterns, not candles, gas lanterns, or torches.
- If you smell gas or suspect a leak, turn off the main gas valve, open all windows, and leave the house immediately. Notify the gas company or the police or fire departments, and do not turn on the lights or do anything that could cause a spark. Do not return to the house until you are told it is safe to do so.
- Your electrical system may be damaged. If you see frayed wiring or sparks, or if you smell something burning (even if you cannot see any fire), immediately shut off the electrical system at the circuit breaker.
- Look for and avoid downed power lines, particularly those in water.
- Do not wade through standing water, which also may contain glass or metal fragments.

Be aware of and avoid hazards, including propane tanks (do not touch them; call the fire department, as they may explode); car batteries (use insulated gloves if you must move one and avoid the acid); chemical spills; and broken glass.

Use Power Safely After a Flood

133

Before beginning any clean-up, call your utility company about using electrical equipment, including power generators. Be aware that it is against the law and a violation of electrical codes to connect generators to your home's electrical circuits without the approved, automatic-interrupt devices. If a generator is on line when electrical service is restored, it can become a major fire hazard. In addition, the improper connection of a generator to your home's electrical circuits may endanger line workers helping to restore power in your area. All electrical equipment and appliances must be completely dry before returning them to service. It is advisable to have a certified electrician check these items if there is any question. Also, remember not to operate any gas-powered equipment indoors.

134 Clean Up Safely After a Flood

- Keep children and pets out of the affected area until cleanup has been completed.
- Wear rubber boots, rubber gloves, and goggles during cleanup.
- Throw out items that cannot be washed and disinfected (mattresses, carpets and rugs and their underpads, upholstered furniture, cosmetics, stuffed animals, baby toys, pillows, foam-rubber items, books, wall coverings, and most paper products).
- Remove and discard drywall and insulation that has been contaminated with sewage or flood waters.
- Thoroughly clean all hard surfaces (such as flooring, concrete, molding, wood and metal furniture, countertops, appliances, sinks, and other plumbing fixtures) with hot water and laundry or dish detergent.

SURVIVAL FACTOID

Floodwaters may contain sewage. Wear gloves and come into as little contact with floodwaters as possible. NEVER allow children to play in floodwaters.

- Help the drying process by using fans, air conditioning units, and dehumidifiers.

135 Clean Yourself Up Afterwards

After completing the cleanup, you will need to wash your hands with soap and warm water. Use water that has been boiled for 1 minute (allow the water to cool before washing your hands) or disinfect water for personal hygiene use. Make a solution of 1/8 teaspoon (0.75 ml) of household bleach per 1 gallon (3.7L) of water. Let it stand for 30 minutes. If the water is cloudy, use a solution of 1/4 teaspoon (1.5 milliliters) of household bleach per 1 gallon (3.7L) of water.

- Wash all clothes worn during the cleanup in hot water and detergent. These clothes should be washed separately from uncontaminated clothes and linens.
- Wash clothes contaminated with flood or sewage water in hot water and detergent. Find a working laundromat for washing large quantities of clothes and linens until your onsite waste-water system has been professionally inspected and serviced.
- Have your onsite waste-water system professionally inspected and serviced if you suspect damage.

Put Together a 72-Hour In-home Emergency Kit   136

Depending on the nature of the disaster, and what is happening in your neighborhood, you may need to shelter in place. **At the very minimum, all homes should have sufficient supplies to last three days following any disaster.** It may take emergency workers some time to reach you, so be prepared to take care of yourself and your family during this period. Assemble your kit in a large backpack or duffle bag so it is portable if necessary, though this kit is designed for survival at home (for Go-Bags, see page xx). Here is a basic list of supplies to keep you going in your home for 72 hours. Make sure to get sufficient supplies for each person in your household.

- Ready-to eat meals (you can purchase these at outdoor supply retailers) for 3 days
- High-energy, non-spoiling snacks such as granola bars or trail mix
- Special foods for infants, children, elderly or those who have special needs
- 1 gallon (3.7 L) of drinking water per person per day,

stored in airtight, non-porous containers
- Water purifying tablets
- Wool blankets
- Sub-zero sleeping bags
- Wool and fleece clothing; extra daily clothing
- First-aid kit
- Hand sanitizer, soap for washing, dish soap
- Wipes
- Toilet paper
- Plastic bags (for clean-up, emergency toilet use, and garbage)
- Toothbrush/toothpaste
- Personal hygiene items (tweezers, nail clippers, etc.)
- Water-proof matches and several disposable lighters
- Candles
- Fire starter kit
- Battery-powered and hand-crank flashlights, extra batteries
- Gloves
- Extra set of car keys
- At least $100 cash in small bills
- Credit cards
- Garbage bags
- Whistle
- Duct tape
- Battery-powered radio (with extra batteries) or crank radio
- Books, magazines, cards or other non-digital entertainment items

137 **Consider Keeping a 7-Day Home Emergency Kit**

I personally highly recommend at least a week's worth of emergency preparedness. Many experts advise having one month's worth of supplies and preparedness, while hard-core preppers usually aim for a year's worth!

138 **Establish Your Emergency Water Supply**

In case of any emergency that could compromise your water supply or if the power goes out and seems likely to stay out for longer than a couple of hours, immediately fill your tubs, sinks, pots, and other containers with fresh, drinkable water. Of course, your 72-hour kit has drinking water supplies, but you'll need water for hygiene and other purposes, so it's wise to have as much as possible. Other water sources include:

- The home hot water tank is a good emergency supply of water during a short-term disaster.
- Snow, rain, and gutter catch basins and rainwater cisterns are excellent ways to collect clean water. Rain and snow water sources are normally safe to use for non-drinking purposes.
-

Purify Water for Drinking

If you run out of the drinking water you previously stored, you must purify water from other sources before drinking it. Boiling is best.

- Boiling: bring water to a full rolling boil for 3 to 5 full minutes, then let cool (at least 30 minutes) before drinking. At altitudes higher than 6,562 feet (2,000 m), boil water for 3 minutes.
- Chemical disinfection: Use chlorine or iodine tablets, following the instructions carefully.
- Pour purified through a coffee filter or cheesecloth to remove any large particles.

Note that these methods will eliminate natural contaminants, such as bacteria, but none of these purification methods will take out man-made chemicals such as dioxin, mercury, windshield washer fluid, or pharmaceuticals. That's why local urban rivers and lakes could be a very bad source for water in a disaster. Be sure to have a proper supply of bottled drinking water.

SURVIVAL FACTOID

Never drink tapwater after a flood. It may be contaminated. Drink only bottled water that has not been compromised.

140 Know When to Evacuate

When local authorities order an evacuation, always follow their instructions. Fires, floods, and hurricanes, among other potential disasters, can and do result in loss of life. Authorities will not ask you to leave your home unless they have reason to believe that you may be in danger. Many tragic examples exist around the world where victims knew that the danger was imminent but chose to ignore official warnings from authorities to evacuate. **If you are ordered to evacuate, do it.**

141 Always Keep Gas in Your Car

Always, at least half a tank. A full tank is better. Gas stations may be closed or have long lines. In a blackout, gas stations may not be able to pump gas.

142 Have a Go Bag Ready

You can purchase a pre-packed bug-out bag from many different online survival sites and outdoors stores, or you can make your own. Keep it under 25 lbs (12 kg) and put it all in a backpack so it is truly portable.

- Copies of your important documents in a waterproof bag (photoIDs, insurance cards, deeds, etc.—see list in tip #TK)
- Extra set of car and house keys
- Copies of credit/ATM cards
- Cash (small bills)
- Bottled water and nonperishable food for 3 days
- Flashlight/extra batteries (LED flashlights last longer than traditional bulbs) or hand-crank flashlight—a high-lumen headlamp will leave your hands free
- Battery-operated radio
- Extra batteries/chargers
- Respirator masks
- A list of the medications each member of your household takes, why they take them, and their dosages. If you store extra medication in your Go Bag,

be sure to refill it before it expires
- First-aid kit
- Toiletries, including wipes
- Change of clothing including climate-appropriate outerwear
- Notepad and pen
- Contact and meeting place information for your household, and a small regional map
- Lightweight raingear and Mylar blanket (If you can fit a sub-zero sleeping bag, do it)
- If you have children, pack child care supplies as well as games and small toys
- If you're older or have any special medical needs, consider including these items:
  - » Instructions and extra batteries for any devices you use
  - » Aerosol tire repair kits and/or tire inflator to repair flat wheelchair or scooter tires
  - » Back-up medical equipment
  - » Items to comfort you in a stressful situation

Pack a Pet Go Bag

143

If you have a pet(s), you will need to pack a pet go-bag as well.

- Copies of medical records that indicate dates of vaccinations and a list of medications your pet takes and why
- Proof of identification and ownership, including copies of registration information, adoption papers, proof of purchase, and microchip information
- Physical description of your pet, including species, breed, age, sex, color, distinguishing traits, and any other vital information about characteristics and behavior plus a photo of you together
- Animal first aid kit, including flea and tick treatment and other items recommended by your veterinarian
- Food and water and dishes, for at least three days
- Collapsible cage or carrier
- Muzzle (non-nylon) and sturdy leash

- Cotton sheet to place over the carrier to help keep your pet calm
- Toys or treats
- Litter, litter pan, and litter scoop
- Plastic bags for clean-up
- Grooming tools

144 Know How to Evacuate

Grab your emergency kit/go bag, your wallet, and cell phone, plus a spare battery or charger. If possible, leave a note telling others when you left and where you are. Shut off water and electricity if officials tell you to do so. Leave natural gas service on unless officials tell you to turn it off. (Only the gas company has to reconnect it, which could take some time.) Plan to use the travel routes specified by local authorities (you know them already, because you reviewed them in your emergency plan rehearsal, right?) If you have time, call or e-mail your out-of-town contact to explain what has happened, who is with you, where you are going, and when you expect to arrive. Take pets with you. Lock your home. Follow instructions from authorities. If you go to an evacuation center, register your personal information at the registration desk. Do not return home until authorities advise that it is safe to do so.

145 Decide Whether to Stay Put or Leave

There may come a time when it might be solely up to you to decide on whether to stay put, hunker down, and "bug in" or to move to a place you consider safer, or "bug out." This is an enormously difficult decision, and one that only you can make.
There are two main factors to consider:

- Do you have somewhere to go that will be safer than staying where you are? Can you get there safely?
- Do you have everything you need for you and your family to survive along the way and if/when you get there?

(Note that for bugging out into the wild, you need training and skills, in addition to being prepared with clothing and a survival kit. If you do not fit the profile of a seasoned outdoor camper, you might want to re-consider bugging out to the wild unless the dangers of staying put are unbearable and leave you no choice.) Ideally, you have prepared for both staying put and bugging out, and you can make the decision based on your assessment of the situation as it unfolds.

Choose a Bug-out Location in Advance

146

Long before you decide to bug out from a disaster, you need to have chosen a potential site—and an alternative, in case your first choice is not available. These potential sites will depend on the scenario, your location, and your method of transport. Potential bug out sites can include a second home or cottage, RV, the home of a relative or friend, a known emergency shelter, a local or national parks, hotel or motel, community emergency recreation center or church. Make sure your family members have rehearsed all survival plans, and know the rules and plans for bugging out. It's conceivable that if disaster strikes, they could be at different locations, so plan and account for this!

Make Your Home Ready for Long-Term Survival

147

To make your home a shelter-in-place location for longer than 72 hours, and to ensure that you are fully prepared for long-term, in-home survival, to the list above, add the following:

- Backup generator
- Fuel supply for generator
- Backup power pack/inverter
- Mini backup power for cell phone
- Manual can opener
- Woodstove or wood fireplace
- Gas fireplace with pilot ignition
- Hardwoods wood supply

- Ultraviolet heaters
- Magic Heat or fondue can for cooking
- Propane for barbeque
- Campstove and fuel (to be used outdoors only!)
- Waterless chemical portable toilet
- Bucket for toilet flushing (use non-drinkable outside water source)
- Candles (12-hour)
- Waterproof matches and BBQ igniters with extra fuel
- Full first aid kit
- Long-term supplies of medications
- Instant heat hand/foot warmers
- Wind-up AM/FM radio
- Bug-Out Survival Kit (see page xx)
- Maps of local area with safe sites marked
- Compass

148 Equip Country Houses, Cottages, Cabins, and RVs

Any home that you own or rent, or an RV that you live in while traveling, should be as well equipped as your main home, especially if planned for use as a bug-out location.

149 Recognize Your Dependency on Electricity

Many folks have no idea just how reliant they are on electricity. They may not realize that their natural gas furnace requires electricity, as does a well pump, or even a gas fireplace (unless it has a manual pilot light.) They may be shocked to discover that during a power blackout, an apartment building's water flow shuts off, emergency hall lighting (if there is any) lasts for only a day or two, and electric-powered heating and cooking equipment is rendered useless. Elevators can become traps and the only way out is a long trek down a dark staircase. For the very young, seniors, and those with disabilities, lack of power may quickly become a life-threatening situation. As part of your emergency readiness, make a point of evaluating your particular power needs. See tips #TK to #TK for back-up power suggestions.

Get Back-up Power

Every area suffers from the occasional blackout, but if you live in a place where the power grid is iffy and outages are routine, or if you are concerned about potential power outages caused by weather or even terrorism, you should consider getting back-up power in the form of a generator. There are two types of generators, the smaller, portable type and the larger, standby type.

Understand a Portable Generator

The portable type has to be started up manually when the power goes out, and it runs on fuel, such as gasoline, that will need to be kept on hand. When the power goes out, it will need to be fueled, started up, and attached to the circuit needing power. A portable generator MUST BE KEPT OUTSIDE least 10 feet (3 m) away from the house, in an open-walled enclosure or under a shelter that protects the generator from the elements but allows full and free circulation of air. It is much less expensive than a standby generator and a good choice if you have occasional outages. Note that portable generators tend to be noisy (except for digital sinewave models.) A standby generator runs on propane or natural gas, and is permanently connected to the home's power circuits, so it automatically comes on when the power goes out; it is a much more expensive option but easier to use, and can power an entire home. Portable generators come in manual and digital models.

Understand a Standby Generator

A standby generator must be professionally installed and maintained. Consider one of these if your area undergoes frequent outages or if sustained loss of power to your home would cause serious problems for your family. Some models come with remote-control handheld units, which come in handy when weather is bad!

153   Consider Digital Portable Generator (AKA an Inverter Generator)

If you need a reliable, low-noise portable generator, the newer digital sine-wave generators are excellent, for the following reasons:

- They are encased in a muffler-like casing, and are very quiet.
- They will work with lithium batteries.
- They produce a clean, stable flow of electricity, safe even for (most) sensitive electronics.
- They won't blow the electrical panel
- They have an enviro-eco switch to reduce fuel consumption.
- They run wattage based on what's needed, not the minimum 50% that conventional models use.

154   Choose the Right Fuel for a Portable Generator

Portable generators can utilize many types of fuels, including gasoline, diesel, propane, vegetable oil (usually requires a conversion of one of the other types), and hydrogen. Factors in making a choice include cost and availability of fuel types, length of run-time with a tank, and wear and tear on the engine. Gasoline and diesel are the most popular, however, to avoid having to refuel (run-times vary from 5 to 12 hours per tank), opt for propane, as large propane tanks can give long, uninterrupted run times. There is the added cost of the propane tanks, and servicing of the tank and generator by a gas fitter. There are newer hydrogen generators now widely available (they use distilled water as fuel!), however, they are very expensive.

155   Get a Pull Start

Buy a portable generator that has a pull-start, in addition to an electronic start. Where there's an electronic start, there's also a small internal battery that needs to be charged at all times, and replaced every few years. With an additional pull-start, a dead battery will not be a problem.

Never Plug the Generator into a Wall Outlet

156

Known as "backfeeding," this is an extremely dangerous practice. It bypasses any built-in household protection devices, can cause a serious fire, endangers your neighbors, and can electrocute any hydro technicians working on nearby lines.

Install an Inlet

157

A very important tip is to have a power transfer switch on "inlet" installed on the home's exterior, which goes directly to the home's electrical panel. You must have a qualified electrician install a power transfer switch.

Hook Up an Extra Tank to a Gasoline-powered Generator

158

For gasoline generators, you can have a second gas can hooked up as an ancillary unit, making it easy to switch up versus re-filling the generator.

Choose the Correct Generator Wattage for Your Space and Usage

159

To understand your usage needs, add up the wattage from all your necessary devices and appliances—this will provide a sense of how much power you need to keep your home running. Then choose a generator that can easily handle that amount. An electrician can help with this task.

Know Your Generator's Peak Wattage and Stay Below It

160

Remember, generators have running watts, and peak watt outputs—stay at the running wattage and under the peak. For example, a 1,000-watt generator is usually happier at 800 watts, and might simply shut off when the 1,000-watts peak is approached.

161 Plug Appliances Directly into the Generator

Or use a heavy duty, outdoor-rated extension cord that is rated (in watts or amps) at least equal to the sum of the connected appliance loads. Check the full length of the cord to ensure it has no cuts or tears. Only use a plug has all three prongs, especially a grounding pin.

162 Understand Standby Generator Systems

Permanent standby generators come in kilowatt sizes, starting at 1 kW to 10+ kW. They can be hooked up to natural gas or propane. They are wired in to the home directly, and sensors turn the unit on when there is a power failure. This is an advantage, if, for example, you are away from home when the power goes out, in which case this feature can save a fridge and freezer full of food from spoilage. Cost of installation may be as much as the price of the unit, or more. In recent major widespread power disruptions, the natural gas services were also disrupted. Propane is more expensive, but also more reliable, whereas natural gas tends to be readily available and cheaper. However, many communities and rural areas do not have natural gas available, leaving propane as the only option. Note that some municipalities and urban centers may have bylaws limiting the use of propane fuel tanks.

163 Never Use a Portable Generator Indoors

This includes inside a garage, carport, basement, crawlspace, or other enclosed or partially-enclosed area, even with ventilation. Portable generators give off carbon monoxide. Opening doors and windows or using fans will not prevent carbon monoxide (CO) buildup in the home. **Never use a portable generator indoors.**

164 Follow Generator Safety Rules Strictly

- A portable generator must be kept outside least 10 feet (3 m) away from the house, in an enclosure or under a shelter that protects the generator from the elements but allows free circulation of air.

- CO can't be seen or smelled. The CO emitted from generators can rapidly lead to full incapacitation and death. Even if you cannot smell exhaust fumes, you may still be exposed to CO. If you start to feel sick, dizzy, or weak while using a generator, get to fresh air immediately: DO NOT DELAY.
- Always have working, battery-operated carbon monoxide and smoke detectors in the home and any other living space where you are operating a generator .
- A garage or shed holding a generator MUST NOT be directly connected to the home or any building housing people, because CO seepage can occur, and can be fatal. Operate it only well away from windows, doors, and vents that could allow fumes to enter the home.
- Never overload the generator.
- Keep generators away from all flammables, including and especially the fuel source! Store fuel for the generator in an approved safety can. Consult your local fire department for local regulations. Store fuel outside, away from living areas, in a locked shed or other protected area. Never store fuel near a fuel-burning appliance, such as a natural gas water heater in a garage. Spilled fuel and invisible vapors from the fuel can be ignited by an appliance's pilot light or electric switches in the appliance.
- Make sure that the open-walled shed or enclosure holding the generator is located "high and dry." To protect the generator from moisture, operate it on a dry surface under an open canopy-like structure, such as under a tarp held up on poles.
- To avoid electrocution, keep the generator dry and do not use in rain or wet conditions.
- Service the unit at least on an annual basis. Test it out regularly.

Convert a Generator to Use Vegetable Oil

165

Many survivalists and preppers opt for alternate fuels, such as used vegetable oils, also known as Waste Vegetable Oil (WVO) to run their generators. This is eco-friendly, less expensive, and less flammable—and will still be available if there is a fossil-fuel shortage. A manual generator can be converted to use vegetable oils, either pure or bio-diesel.

166 Use a Car as a Back-up Generator

A car can provide temporary emergency back-up power with the use of an inverter pack that converts the DC to AC. It won't generate a lot of power, but it can power a light, recharge a solar battery bank, boost a dead generator, and charge a cell phone.

167 Go Solar

Let the sun provide for your minor power needs. There are a variety of small, portable "plug 'n' play" solar systems, with folding and flexible panels, and/or tripods with standard rigid panels. Flexi-panels roll up, and can be taken with you to use wherever you may be, whether you set them up on the roof of a vehicle or simply lay them on the ground outdoors on a camping trip. Plug 'n' play solar systems provide ease of setup and use, as well as safety, since they have their own internal fuse switches and safety overload sensors. You can power cell phone batteries, GPS units, flashlights, and lights using solar power. You do have to rotate panels to maximize solar input and of course, keep snow off them. Some high-efficiency panels will produce wattage even on cloudy days. Should a solar system run dry due to over-use or lack of sunlight, it can be connected to a generator, via a car battery charger, to your bank of solar batteries. Ask a professional certified electrician to inspect or assist with hooking up the solar system. I ignored this tip on my first try, and after reversing the battery hookups by mistake, I heard a loud bang, and blew up a $200 inverter. It could have been much worse.

> "
> *The ache for home lives in all of us, the safe place where we can go . . . "*
> —Maya Angelou

Get the Best Solar Batteries

168

Lithium solar batteries are the most efficient.

Get Long-term Food Provisions

169

If you are going to prep for a long-term survival situation, you'll need more than the MREs (Meals, Ready-to-eat) or other short-term nutrition in your 72-hour kit. Survival foods should be easy to prepare and non-perishable, and provide good nutrition, including carbohydrates and fats. Good options can be found among canned foods, bulk foods, military ration packs, and camping instant meal packs. Also consider soup mixes, trail mix, granola bars, peanut butter, pastas, rice, beans, jerky, and hard cheeses. Avoid refined sugary foods, which do not provide either sustained energy or much in the way of nutritive value. There are many on-line survival prepper and bulk food meal sites where you can stock up on supplies. Also, bulk food wholesalers and restaurant suppliers have good prices and product variety.

Keep Up Personal Hygiene

170

Cleanliness and hygiene are important aspects of survival, both physically (to avoid illness and infection) and for psychological reasons. Washing your hands frequently and well is crucial for avoiding illness and infection. In general, people touch their faces hundreds of times per day, and if your hands are not clean, bacteria and viruses will easily be transmitted. Keep extra water for washing, and make sure to pack hand sanitizer and disinfecting wipes in your kit.

- In a pinch, you can clean your body using wipes
- Rainwater can be collected in clean containers and used for bathing
- For longer-term survival or off-grid, camping retailers offer portable showers that run on propane/butane with a large stainless steel canister that holds 2 or 3 gallons of water, and has either a manual pressure pump or battery-powered pump, and include a shower nozzle

and hose attachment
- Wash your hands frequently or use hand sanitizer

171 Pack Hand Sanitizer

Hand sanitizer is essential for quick clean ups. Additionally, hand sanitizer that is alcohol based can also be used as a fire starter. You should include several bottles of hand sanitizer in your at-home kit as well as your bug-out kit.

172 Manage Waste

In a survive-at-home situation, if you cannot access a working toilet, standard or chemical, you will have to improvise.

If you can go outside:

- Dig a hole in a location that is far from your living area yet reasonably accessible
- Be sure to cover waste matter with a layer of earth

If you cannot go outside:

- Use plastic bags for defecation; seal loosely and dispose in a metal can with a tight-fitting lid
- A soon as you can do so safely, bury them outside, reasonably far from your living site

173 Dispose of Garbage

Have a plan in place for disposing of garbage. Re-use as much as possible, including composting if you can. You will need trash cans with tight-fitting lids to store garbage until you can permanently dispose of it. Your main options for getting rid of refuse are burning and burying.

174 Stock Up on Medications

For disaster preparedness, always have extra supplies of medications on hand, especially prescription medications.

If and when disaster strikes, it is likely that pharmacies will be closed and useless due to power outage and/or anarchy. For special conditions such as asthmas or diabetes, this is particularly important. Know the medications you and your family require on a regular a basis and be sure to have a supply in your long-term survival kit.

Install a Woodstove for Heat and Cooking

A large rectangular box-like woodstove with a large BTU capacity will ensure that you have heat and can cook food if you are sheltering in place for a long time. It will require a double-walled insulated chimney. Hire a wood heating-approved technician to ensure correct installation with appropriate wall and ceiling clearances, and underpadding.

Use a thermometer attached to the stovepipe front to indicate danger zones for heat, utilize cleaning logs, clean chimney regularly, empty the ash drawer daily, and burn clean woods. Wood fireplace inserts are also excellent for emergency heating. Make sure you have an upgraded chimney liner, for safety and efficiency.

There are other options for long-term, off-grid heating and cooking. Check out prepper websites to find out more.

Survival Story

During a large-scale, lengthy blackout, one family set up their camping tent in the living room near the fireplace, and indoor-camped there! They sealed off all the other rooms in their home to conserve heat.

Burn the Right Wood

In general, the rule is for heating output, use hardwoods, and for flame, use softwoods. Never burn pressure-treated wood or lumber. Avoid cedar, which sparks dangerously. Poplar tends to be waterlogged. Avoid green, non-seasoned wood. If possible, avoid evergreen woods such as pine, as these woods produce creosote, which builds up in the chimney piping, and can ignite. Good woodstove choices include ironwood, oak, sugar maple, hickory and beech; birch is great when its seasoned properly. Keep a working fire extinguisher nearby, and as well as working smoke and carbon monoxide detectors.

177   Install a Thermo-electric Stove Fan for Heat

These woodstove fans are excellent since they don't require electricity to work. They have a built-in thermo-coupler that uses the heat from the woodstove to produce electricity, which propels the fan blades to circulate heat to the room area.

178   Opt for Propane-fueled Appliances

Propane cookstoves, refrigerators, and furnaces are readily available, common in rural areas where there is no available natural gas, and often used in RVs. They are very effective, and work even in a power outage, as long as they have a pilot light start-up. They tend to be very expensive, and must be certified, installed, and repaired by a certified gas fitter. When not serviced or installed properly, they can blow up.

179   Secure Your Home

Your home should be a place of safety and security in good times and challenging times. A secure home does not offer easy entry to thieves or other criminals, and it can be defended if necessary. Take the following steps to make your home unappealing to those who have no business there:

- Install solid-core or metal-clad doors instead of flimsy hollow-core models
- Use a floor bolt to secure sliding glass entry doors
- Use quality window locks or install special models that allow windows to open no more than a few inches
- Choose good-quality deadbolt locks for all outer doors
- Install an alarm system that connects to the local police station
- Put up signs or stickers on windows and doors even if you do not have a security system

Don't Hide a Key

180

Never hide an extra key under a doormat or rock—give it to a trusted neighbor or local friend instead.

Lock Up Every Time

181

Whenever you leave the house, lock the door behind you— even if you're just stepping out into the hallway of your apartment building or your own yard.

Close the Windows

182

And lock them. Never leave windows unlocked or open when you go out. If you have window air conditioner units, install them with brackets, bolts, or sliding locks so that intruders cannot push them in or our to gain entry to your home.

Secure the Garage

183

Unlocked garage doors and doors that lead into the house from the garage must never be left open or unlocked.

Install a Panic Room

184

Consider installing a "panic room," which is a fortified room where family members can shelter or hide in case of natural disasters or human intruders. Reinforced walls and ceilings, a separate ventilation system, and communications equipment are the hallmarks of a panic room.

Build a Fallout Shelter

185

Hardcore preppers plan for the very worst, which means a blast and/or fallout shelter. Instructions are beyond the scope of this book, but you can find them online and in many books.

SURVIVE AT WORK

CHAPTER 3

SURVIVE AT WORK

When you think of survival skills in the workplace, your mind probably jumps to problems like meeting a difficult deadline or handling an abusive boss rather than what you would do in the event of an emergency situation or natural disaster while you were at work. Yet, as you know from the earlier chapters in this book, a survival mindset means being aware that disasters can and do happen anytime, anywhere, without regard for your personal convenience. In fact, since the typical full-time worker spends one-third of his or her life at work, or commuting, it's quite likely that you could be at work or on your way to or from work when disaster strikes. This chapter will offer tips to help you survive long enough

> " *It's a very sobering feeling to be up in space and realize that one's safety factor was determined by the lowest bidder on a government contract.* "
> —**Alan Shepard**

to get yourself safely out of the workplace, so that you can go home or bug out, as needed—and perhaps help the business survive, too.

File a Copy of Your Personal Emergency Information Form with HR

186

No matter where you work, you should fill out an emergency information form and file it in an easily accessible place at your workspace. If your place of work is large enough to have an HR department, you will likely have done this when you signed on If your workplace does not have an HR department or an staff member who maintains this information, adapt the form on page xx and file it yourself. Keep the form in an obvious place so that emergency personnel can find it. If you work as a freelancer or consultant, your emergency information wallet card can fulfill this purpose.

Know the Workplace Emergency Plans

187

Find out what emergency plans are in place. If you work in an office building or commercial space, there is probably a fire and/or evacuation plan, and there may be regular drills. Pay attention when these happen, and know the locations of fire extinguishers, first aid kits, and at least 2 different emergency exits. If you work in a high-rise, the safer plan may be to shelter-in-place. It is your responsibility to ensure that you know the risks and learn proper safety routines in case of power outage; natural disaster such as fire, flood, or earthquake; or violent attack. If your workplace does not have emergency protocols, it is up to you to develop the plans. Approach your supervisor and other staff members to create an office plan just like your home plan, for safely responding to disaster. Just as you did with your home, ask yourself, "What can happen at work?" Is the location of your workplace subject to any potential natural disasters such as flooding, earthquakes, or weather events such as tornadoes? Do you work in a place that might attract a violent attack of any kind? Make sure the plan is distributed to all workers and posted in a prominent location.

188 Assign Emergency Tasks

The first line of prevention and response in a workplace emergency comes from the workers themselves. Make sure employees have assigned duties, such as alerting staff in case of fire, assisting those who require help in evacuating, operating fire extinguishers, and providing first aid.

189 Train Employees in Emergency Medical Responses

Every workplace should offer employees classes in first aid procedures. At the very least, employers should be sure that at least one employee is trained in basic first aid techniques, knows how to provide CPR and use an automated external defibrillator (AED), and is trained in health and safety specifications particular to the business.

SURVIVAL FACTOID

Disaster Doesn't Discriminate
During the massive 2003 "Northeast Blackout," which left some 45 million Americans and 10 million Canadians without power for periods ranging from a day to nearly a week, many people who normally enjoy plenty of resources ended up sleeping on park benches and in other public places. Credit and debit cards were of no use. Cell phones worked only sporadically. The lesson? Disaster eliminates advantages.

190 Check the First Aid Kit

Be sure your workplace does have a basic first-aid kit that is fully stocked. This should be checked and re-filled annually. A sign should be placed prominently indicating where the kit can be found.

191 Update Sprinkler Systems

Ensure the building's sprinkler systems are operational.

Larger businesses will usually be subject to regulatory checks, but smaller businesses should check with the local fire department. If the business is in an area subject to freezing, there should also be a sprinkler turn-off plan.

Evacuate in Response to an In-Office Hazard

192

If the problem occurs in the workplace itself or inside the building, for example, smoke conditions or a known fire, a chemical spill, or a bomb threat, employees should evacuate. Practicing an orderly departure in advance will improve the likelihood of a real-life scenario unfolding well.

Shelter in Place During Severe Weather

193

In the event of severe weather, such as a damaging storm, hurricane, or tornado, employees should move to the most structurally sound part of the building, far away from exterior glass. A flood requires moving to higher floors; the second or third floor may not be high enough—a tsunami can send water very high very rapidly, so go higher.

Prepare Your Workplace for an Earthquake

194

If your place of work is in an earthquake zone, the building and/or business owners should ensure that the building is up to local seismic safety standards, address any structural vulnerabilities, and make needed repairs promptly. In the United States, the Federal Emergency Management Agency (FEMA) publishes structural guidelines to be followed to maximize building safety. Nonstructural items must be anchored, braced, reinforced, or otherwise secured. Earthquake drills should be practiced in advance, with clear instructions for safe places to "drop, cover, and hold on" (see page xx) and when to evacuate.

Assemble a 72-Hour Workplace Emergency Kit

195

While the average home usually has at least a few pieces of basic emergency gear, such as a flashlight or extra blankets, most workplaces, offices, and commercial environments have zilch in the way of emergency gear, outside of a standard first aid kit. In addition to the basic first-aid kit, a well-stocked office or workplace emergency kit should contain have supplies to allow the entire staff to shelter-in-place for 72 hours. Use this checklist.

- 1 gallon (3.7 L) of water per person per day, stored in airtight, non-porous containers
- Ready-to eat meals (you can purchase these at outdoor supply retailers) for 3 days
- High-energy, non-perishable snacks
- Mylar "space" blankets
- Hand sanitizer
- Flashlight (powerful, hand-cranked or battery-powered, with extra batteries); headlamp is ideal
- Glow sticks in case of gas leakages (glow sticks can safely provide light when flashlights and candles cannot be used)
- Whistle
- Duct tape
- Crank or battery-powered radio (with extra batteries)
- Battery-powered phone charger (with extra batteries)
- Dust masks
- Back-up power (a portable generator makes sheltering in place much more comfortable)

196 Put Together a Personal Workplace Go-Bag

To be completely prepared, you will want your own personal workplace emergency bag that can do double-duty as a go-bag or a stay-put bag. Start with a large, waterproof backpack that you can carry when full, and that will fit under your desk or someplace close so you can easily grab it if needed.

- Extra set of home and car keys
- Copy of your ID
- Cell phone charger, crank or battery-powered, with extra batteries
- Money, a small stash of cash hidden in your bag
- Water, a gallon (3.7 L) stored in hydration packs

- Food, non-perishable, high-energy items
- Flashlight that is small, powerful, and battery-powered
- Emergency radio for information and communication, such as a crank or battery-powered emergency radio
- Extra batteries
- Space blanket or small woolen blanket
- Whistle to signal for help
- Sensible shoes to wear instead of work shoes that may not be suitable for running or distance walking (bring an old pair of sneakers or hiking shoes)
- First aid kit: small and portable
- Poncho: to protect from rain and snow
- Local map
- Multitool knife

 We cannot stop natural disasters but we can arm ourselves with knowledge: so many lives wouldn't have to be lost if there was enough disaster preparedness."
—**Petra Nemcova**

Save Your Business

197

If you own the business, you owe it to yourself to also have a business survival plan as well as a personal survival plan, so that all your hard work is not lost during a temporary emergency such as a major power outage. Would your business survive a prolonged period of downtime? Can your employees can work remotely? What are the possible consequences to your business from a major disruption? Will it survive the increased expenses of recovery or repairs? You will want to ensure that your business has adequate insurance against fire, flood, and likely natural and/or human disasters? When you are making your plan, be sure to address the following key considerations:

- Evacuation and relocation off-site
- Backup lighting and generator
- Backup computer systems
- Security company

- Short and long-term disaster and/or power outage
- Employee/staff safety and survival
- Business interruption contingencies
- Business sabotage contingencies
- Cyberspace attack preparedness
- When to shut down protocols

198 Plan for Digital Security

Does your business have a comprehensive back-up plans for all computer systems and databases? Think about the best way to protect your business secrets and know-how, so you don't have to start over from scratch.

199 Get a Professional Security Consultation

If you are a business owner, you might want to consult with a professional security company or hire one to formulate appropriate plans for your business's protection, including such risks as corporate espionage and cyber-attacks.

200 Heed Public Alerts

Increasingly, violent attacks upon workplaces, schools, or in public locations, once unthinkable, have become a terrifying reality. If your area has a heightened danger alert or warning of an attack, close down temporarily until the alert is removed.

201 Practice Lockdown

Though violent public attacks remain thankfully rare, it is important to have a lockdown plan in place and to practice it. Lockdowns become necessary when an intruder with violent intention enters a building. Seconds count in these situations, so practice is essential. The goal of the lockdown is to protect the people in the building from harm by hiding or barricading themselves away from the intruder.

> " *It was a bad day at the office.*"
> —Anonymous

Follow Lockdown Procedure

If a lockdown is necessary:

- Make a lockdown announcement.
- Clear everyone from hallways into rooms.
- Assist those who need help into rooms.
- Close and lock all windows and doors.
- Close window coverings, cover door windows with paper.
- Block door with furniture, if appropriate.
- Group people in a part of the room that cannot be seen from outside and is not in potential lines of fire.
- Turn lights off.
- Lie on the floor, keeping away from doors and windows.
- Keep silent. Turn off the ringer on all cell phones.
- If a fire alarm has been activated, do not evacuate unless fire or smoke is visible.

Be Conscious of Inherent Workplace Dangers

Workplace disasters result in thousands of deaths every year. Typical workplace accidents are caused by inadequate training, ignoring safety protocols, equipment failures, improper maintenance, chemical spills or accidents (mislabeling of containers, e.g.), failure to wear proper eye or body protection, lack of protective clothing or footwear, vehicle accidents, and explosions. Follow government- regulated workplace health and safety standards, safe workplace chemical usage standards, and mandatory workplace training and certifications. Does your workplace follow safety and disaster protocols? Do you have adequate first aid kits, safety showers, emergency equipment, and personnel trained in first aid? Most workplace accidents can be prevented.

CHAPTER 4

SURVIVE IN THE WILDERNESS

SURVIVE IN THE WILDERNESS

SURVIVE IN THE WILDERNESS

HOW TO START A FIRE WITH WATER

Chapter 5

SURVIVE IN THE WILDERNESS

If you've gotten this far in this book then you already know that the best advice is to be so well prepared that you never find yourself in a do-or-die survival situation—and good preparation is particularly important when venturing into the great outdoors. Nature can be unpredictable, however, and there will be times when bad luck and/or unforeseeable circumstances land even the best prepared of adventurers in a challenging situation. What should you do if find yourself with a broken down vehicle in a remote location or realize that your planned short hike has taken a wrong turn and you're completely lost in the woods with the sun about to set? Do you know how to find shelter, make fire, get drinking water and something to eat?

> " *I grew up in the north woods of Canada. You had to know certain things about survival. Wilderness survival courses weren't very formalized when I was growing up, but I was taught certain things about what to do if I got lost in the woods."*
> —Margaret Atwood"

How will you communicate your predicament to rescuers? In order to stay alive until you are rescued or find your way to safety, read the tips in this chapter to help you make the right choices to get out of trouble.

Plan Ahead

Before you go on any nature adventure, take the time to plan your trip properly. A smart trip plan covers the following:

1. Route: Choose a route that is appropriate to the age, experience, and fitness of all the people going on your trip. Map it out day by day carefully, noting sources of water, camping locations, and where to find assistance.
2. Maps: Bring paper maps (note: plural) as well as digital, including at least one that is waterproof or in a waterproof container.
3. Gear: Bring appropriate gear for your trip in a pack that you can comfortably carry, with proper equipment for any specific activities you expect to engage in.
4. Water/Food: Pay particular attention to your water needs. There are many online calculators that will help you determine precisely how much water you need per person depending on the activity level. Note sources of replenishment on your maps.
5. Communication: Smart hikers bring reliable communication equipment and file detailed trip plans.
6. Weather: Time your trip to good weather (e.g., don't plan to walk Asian jungles during monsoon season), and monitor the weather constantly during your adventure, adjusting plans as needed.
7. Emergencies: Bring a first-aid kit and an emergency kit.

205 | Acquire Basic Outdoor Skills

If you want to enjoy the outdoors regularly and safely, it is smart to make a real effort to learn basic outdoor skills by taking practical, hands-on classes, and keeping your skills up through frequent practice. Basic outdoor skills everyone would benefit from include:

- Navigation and orientation skills
- How to tie basic knots
- How to build a fire
- How to build a simple shelter
- Basic first aid skills
- How to filter water
- How to recognize and prepare edible plants and insects

206 | File a Trip Itinerary

Before you go, fill out a trip itinerary and leave a copy for at least one reliable relative or friend, and, if possible, file another copy with local park officials. See the appendix (page xx) for an example you can customize. Trip itineraries allow you to review your planned trip and route, as well as your gear and supplies. Leaving trip plans with responsible parties (who are not traveling with you) greatly increases your chances of being located by search and rescue. Stay on your initial trip route, and refrain from changing the plans at the last minute.

207 | Pack a Survival Kit

If you intend to go out and enjoy nature beyond the confines of your backyard or the local park, you must have a good survival and safety kit on your person at all times **in addition to your normal trekking gear.** The survival kit should be customized based on the type of wilderness excursion; the length and difficulty of the trip; whether you will be on land or water, in the desert or forest; and how much weight and size are you willing and able to carry comfortably. The ideal container for a full survival kit is a waterproof backpack. The categories of items in the kit will align with basic survival requirements: shelter, fire, water, signaling, food, first aid, navigation, communication, and specifics for the outdoor activities. Be sure to get sufficient supplies for the number of people going on the trip.

Pack a Basic Survival Kit

208

If you need a minimal kit due to space constraints or for a very brief trip through non-remote territory, bring:

- a high-carbon steel knife with a 6- to 10-inch (15 to 25 cm) blade
- a small firestarter kit (flint rod/magnesium; waterproof matches, and/or butane lighter)
- a tin can
- 8 x10 foot (2.5 x 3 m) heavy duty nylon tarp with reinforced grommets
- high-energy foodstuffs such as trail mix
- first-aid kit

Pack a Long-term Survival Kit

209

Use this checklist for a fully stocked survival kit that will keep you alive until you are rescued:

- tarp or sheet of plastic 8 x 10 ft. (2.5 x 3m) or larger
- solar and space blanket
- solar bivouac (bivy) sack, insulated
- paratrooper cord 50 to 100 ft. (15 to 30m)
- duct tape
- orange contractor-type garbage bags
- waterproof and stormproof matches
- "metal match," i.e., flint and a magnesium rod
- butane lighter intended for outdoor use
- steel wool, superfine
- fuel cubes, or cotton ball soaked in petroleum jelly
- 12-hour candles

> " *The more you know, the less you have to carry. The less you know, the more you have to carry.*"
> —**Mors Kochanski**

- watertight tin can for boiling, or sheet of heavy duty aluminum foil
- headlamp, 100+ lumens LED
- chlorine or iodine drops/tablets for water purification
- first aid supplies for top10 situations (burns, bleeding, blisters, fractures, dislocations, insect bites, hypothermia, dehydration, heat exhaustion, and electrolyte imbalance)
- high-energy foods (granola bars, trail mix, jerky)
- large, 6- to 10-inch (15 to 25 cm) knife
- small pocket knife or multitool
- folding saw
- magnetic compass and topographical maps/nautical charts
- GPS handheld unit with maps preloaded
- smartphone and cell booster/amplifier
- tracking locator device or satellite phone
- signal flares and smoke flares
- bear bangers or bear mace (if legal in your jurisdiction)
- air horn
- outdoor pealess whistle (such as a Fox-40)
- signaling mirror
- snare wire
- fishing hooks and line
- glow sticks
- insect repellant and bite treatments

210 Bring Activity Specific Gear

In addition to your survival kit, be certain to bring along appropriate activity-specific gear. For a skiing/ snowboarding trip, for example, add a multitool and repair kit; for snowmobiling or ice fishing, bring an ice pick; for a biking trip, a tire repair kit and multitool; for boating, a puncture kit, extra paddles, baler, and flotation device. Research what is needed and check with experts to make sure you are not leaving out anything important.

211 Bring a Flotation Device for Every Person

If any part of trip includes boating, you must have an

approved, appropriately sized personal flotation device for each member of your party. Make sure everyone wears theirs every time they are in the boat.

Pack a Kid's Survival Kit

212

Children make great hikers; obviously, you must choose your route to be appropriate for the age and experience of each child. Never take risks with children. Each child should have, on their person, the following items:

> **SURVIVAL TIP**
>
> Avoid high-energy protein bars. They freeze in subzero temps, and they do not provide what you really need in a potential starvation situation, which is carbs and fats.

- outdoor whistle (e.g., a Fox40 model)
- rain outfit (ideally, a waterproof jacket and pants) or poncho
- brightly colored clothing
- granola bars
- hydration pack
- if the temperature is low, instant heat packs
- bug repellant
- emergency tracking device

Choose an Appropriate Container for Your Survival Kit

213

If your excursion includes water activities, the survival kit should be packed in a container that is waterproof and floats. Make sure you can carry the kit wherever you go, and that you haven't made it so large, heavy, or unwieldy that you don't feel happy to bring it along on every jaunt. What is the point of preparing if you decide your survival kit is too heavy to put in the canoe when you leave your campsite for a morning paddle, only to find yourself in trouble and without your supplies?

Make Your Own Kit

214

Many people who take my workshops ask, "Do you recommend store-bought survival kits?" With the exception of some high-end aviation industry survival kits, and a very few prepper kits found online, I answer "no." Many pre-packed commercial survival kits are pricey, have poor selections, and contain low quality or useless survival items. It's much better to go through the experience of building your own survival kit, learning how to use everything ahead of time.

215 Check Expiry Dates and Temperature Requirements

Some items in a survival kit do have expiry dates, and for good reason: they may break down over time, and in some cases, such as with flares, may even become dangerous! Additionally, some items, including many prescription drugs, must be stored within specific temperature ranges or they lose efficacy. Check all such items and be sure to store them properly.

216 Take a Wilderness First Aid Class

Your backcountry emergency first aid kit differs from your standard home or office firstaid kit in important ways, most significantly in assuming that professional medical treatment may be a long time or distance away. If you hike or take wilderness trips with any regularity, a firstaid class is a very good idea—if you don't know how to use all the items in your kit, you will be of little use in an emergency. Before any outdoor excursion, do a hazard and risk assessment, and decide what are the most probable accidents and dangers. Learn how to perform the necessary procedures, and design your first aid kit accordingly.

217 Assemble Your Outdoor First Aid Kit

Here is a checklist:

- first aid booklet
- victim survey and first aid history forms (for medics)
- personal medications
- sterile gauze pads and pressure dressings of various

sizes, for bleeding
- burn-dressing, non-adhering pads
- bandages of various shapes and sizes
- butterfly bandages or SteriStrips
- disposable razor
- triangular bandages
- cling wrap
- antibacterial flush, such as Bactine
- antihistamines
- anti-diarrhea tablets
- electrolyte sugar/salt crystals
- insect bite lotions and sprays
- DEET-based insect repellant, or organic (oil of lemon-eucalyptus) based for kids over 3 years old
- NSAID and acetaminophen painkillers
- Cortisone cream
- First-aid tape
- heat and cold packs
- tensor bandages
  space blankets
- small and large garbage bags
- first-aid gloves
- alcohol-based hand sanitizer
- cleansing wipes
- irrigation tool or syringe
- surgical scissors
- tweezers
- CPRmask
- oral thermometer

> **SURVIVAL FACTOID**
>
> I once met a very proud Scout Leader, who showed me his survival kit with great excitement. I noticed that his space blanket had decomposed and crumbled into a powdery substance, becoming completely useless. He hadn't checked it for several years.

Pack a 3-Item Emergency Kit   218

A popular question we get when teaching wilderness survival courses is, "What 3 items are best to have, if that is all you could carry?" Survival experts usually argue about this with great excitement, and while there are many different opinions, my own personal recommendations are:

- a large knife
- a flint sparker
- a tin can

With these, you have the potential for shelter, fire, and drinkable water.

219 Adjust Your Kit for the Terrain and Conditions

For boating or winter activities, add a hypothermia kit, complete with solar blankets, instant heat packs, a wool blanket, a sleeping bag, and a portable butane camp stove, plus high-energy granola bars. For hot or desert activities, include a shade screen, sunscreens and lip balms, and sports drink.

220 Pack a Candy Tin Emergency Kit

Another popular debate that rages is what to put in a survival kit the size of a "cough candy tin." I would recommend a flint and matches, a small pocketknife with saw, and some tin foil to make a boiling can.

221 Acknowledge the Dangers of Adrenaline Rush Pursuits

Extreme outdoor games and activities have become popular, but despite what you see on television, there are serious risks associated with these sports. Outdoor adventure activities such as paragliding, zip-lining, mountain biking, off-piste skiing and snowboarding, ice climbing, and mountain climbing have a higher risk of serious and fatal injury than traditional outdoor activities such as backpacking, canoeing, and camping. Mechanized sports such as ATV-ing, snowmobiling, motor-boating, motorcycling, and off-roading are inherently dangerous. When you add alcohol to speed, recklessness frequently ensues, and the result is all too often fatal. Any combination of aggressiveness, bad weather, variable terrain, low light (such as at night), and failure to be prepared can add up to disaster.

222 Get Acclimatized Before You Go

Physical acclimatization can profoundly improve your chances of survival. Most people have a narrow comfort zone, typically within a few degrees of 68°F (20° C). Before you go out on a wilderness trip, prepare yourself by turning the thermostats down or refraining from air conditioning for several days. Understand how your body will react to the prolonged discomfort of being cold or hot, then plan and equip yourself accordingly.

Dress Appropriately

223

You may have heard the expression "Cotton kills!" It is true that in wet, cold climates, cotton clothing is the worst choice because cotton loses its insulating properties when wet, and takes forever to dry out (you might have noticed how long it takes for wet jeans to dry!) However, for these very same reasons, cotton clothing can be a good choice for a hot climate. The point is to pack and dress appropriately for the specific weather where you are going and the actual activities you are planning.

> **SURVIVAL FACTOID**
>
> Polyester, fleece and Goretex can be extremely flammable. If you are in a survival situation that requires a fire for warmth or cooking, be very careful around open flames.

Consider Survival When Dressing

224

Many outdoor adventurers who are dressed properly for their specific outdoor activity may find, however, if faced with a survival situation, that their clothing and footwear might not make sense. A cross-country skier wearing very lightweight wicking materials could be in trouble if stuck outdoors overnight, while a desert hiker wearing shorts and a cotton t-shirt will similarly find this outfit does not work for a desert sleepover. In survival scenarios, these activity-specific clothing choices could be disastrous. An extra layer than can be added or removed is a good idea.

Wear or Bring Bright Colors

225

Brightly colored clothing makes you more visible. This is ideal if searchers are looking for you, and it is often the law during hunting season to wear bright orange clothing. Even if you do not wish to wear neon clothing, it is a good idea to bring at least one item that is brightly colored enough to be seen through tress and vegetation or from a long distance away or above.

226 **Layer in Any Weather**

The most important concept when choosing clothing for outdoor adventures is layering. There are two main reasons why layering is smart. Firstly, no matter the activity, layering gives you choices, allowing you to add or subtract for comfort. Secondly, and more important for survival, layers trap air, and air is a good insulator.

227 **Use 3 Layers for Winter**

For winter activities, dress in three layers:

- Base layer—long underwear that fits snugly and is made of a wicking material such as a synthetic or performance fabric (nylon, spandex, various polyester blends), silk, or lightweight wool (merino is a good choice). Wicking materials transfer moisture from your skin out to the outer layer, where it evaporates, keeping you dry and warm. Nonwicking fabrics like cotton retain moisture (from sweat, for example) and conduct needed heat away from your body.
- Insulating layer—designed to trap heat close to your body, the insulation layer should be a lofty material such as fleece, down (keep it dry), or wool. Looser fitting garments are best for this middle layer.
- Outer layer—also called the shell layer, this should be a wind and waterproof layer that protects you from the elements; GoreTex, ripstop nylon, or polyurethane-coated nylon are good choices.

228 **Opt for 2 Layers in the Heat**

Hot conditions call for layers, too.

- Base layer—choose smooth, closefitting synthetic underwear. Nylon or poly blends are good choices.
- Outer layer—loose-fitting clothing helps air flow, and full-coverage, UPF-rated garments are ideal. You want to be protected from the sun. In dry heat, cotton's moisture-retaining habits work to your benefit, as when sweat evaporates more slowly, you stay cooler longer. In hot and humid conditions, however, you choose lightweight polyester and nylon garments.

> **SURVIVAL FACTOID**
>
> To discourage stinging and biting insects, choose light and earth-tone colors, and avoid contrasting colors.

Get Expert Clothing Advice

229

When shopping for nature adventure clothing, go to a reputable outdoor equipment retailer or do your research online to understand the best options for the temperatures and conditions you are likely to encounter (dry and cold requires different choices than humid and cold, for example), in order to choose the best clothing options.

Wear a Hat

230

A lid is crucial in every scenario. In the sunshine and heat, a hat blocks damaging sunlight, and helps to prevent heat exhaustion or heatstroke. Choose a hat made of UPF-rated material that breathes and fully shades your face and neck. In cold weather, when you can lose nearly 50% of your body heat through your head, a warm woolen or fleece hat is a necessity.

Protect Your Face

231

In extreme cold, bring headgear that covers the face, such as a balaclava, or a separate fleece facemask to keep your face warm and prevent frostbite.

Protect Your Eyes

232

Always bring good quality sunglasses on any outdoor

excursion. For snow conditions, protective UV goggles or sunglasses are necessary. Water activities call for lightweight sunglasses with polarized lenses. Visit a reputable outdoor retailer to choose the right ones. It is wise to have a spare set, as sunglasses are prone to accidents and loss. Always bring a spare pair.

233 Bring Multiple Forms of Sunscreen

The best bets are physical barrier-type sunscreens with zinc oxide or titanium dioxide as the main ingredients. Bring a waxy stick as well as a lotion; apply before you go out and reapply at least twice during the day and after swimming.

234 Treat Your Feet Well

Socks should be made of wicking fabrics such as wool (best, as it is antimicrobial as well as wicking) or polyester blend (wicking but no antibacterial properties.) No cotton socks, ever! Socks must fit perfectly. Bunching is a recipe for blisters. Blisters can be disastrous, leading at best to pain and misery and at worst to infection.

235 Splurge on Footwear

Choose the best quality footwear you can afford. For hiking and backpacking, choose waterproof hiking boots with ankle support and good traction (such as those with a Vibram-type sole). For all serious walking or hiking trips, good hiking boots or shoes are a necessity.

236 Buy the Best Boots

If you wish to enjoy outdoor pursuits in winter weather, you should purchase the best-quality boots you can afford. For winter activities, insulated, waterproof boots with good traction are a must. Do not scrimp. Find a reputable outdoor retailer and ask for advice. Make sure you have a good fit.

Use Plastic Bags Against Leaks

237

If your boots are leaky, place plastic bags over your socks before slipping feet into boots.

Stay in Communication

238

Although one of the pleasures of being out in nature lies in not communicating with the world back home, it's foolish to cut yourself off completely. Communications technology is a gift to those who enjoy the outdoors—it allows adventurers to provide a location in case they get lost, and enables them to call for help in case of emergency. Never go out without some reliable form of communication!

Use a Tracker

239

Tracking devices work via satellite, and some can pair via Bluetooth with a cell phone. Most models allow for prerecorded messages to be sent out to selected recipients, for example to convey that "everything is okay." They also have emergency 911 or SOS buttons to be used in case of serious emergencies. With certain kinds of trackers, your travels can be followed online, allowing selected people to see your location in real time whenever the unit is activated. You will have to pay for the device itself, plus an annual activation fee to keep it working. If you are uncertain of your wilderness navigation skills, traveling with children, or going to treacherous locations, one of these devices may be a lifesaver.

Communicate Via Radio

240

Another way to stay in communication with others on your trip or off is to use General Mobile Radio Service (GMRS) walk-ie-talkies. These 2-way communication devices vary in price, with less expensive models offering a limited range, especially in the outdoors, and more pricey versions with a wider signal range. Some hand held GPS units have built in GMRS radios; when you pair them up and call the other party, they automatically transmit your latitude and longitude position.

241 On the Water, Use VHF

For boating, ham radios and VHS/VHF radios are widely used to communicate with a marine or other base. They use a particular radio frequency range to transmit and receive signals, and to communicate with harbors and marinas, bridges and locks, as well as to request rescue services. Do not go on a boating trip without a working radio of this type, and practice operating it before you go.

242 Use a Satellite Phone for Communication

The most reliable (and most expensive) mobile communications device is the satellite phone, which will send and receive in most regions on the planet. Satellite phones bypass the land-based cellular network completely, instead communicating via satellites that are either stationary or in low Earth orbit. There are units for regional and for international use; in either case, the unit itself is costly, and there is a per minute charge for usage. If you are traveling to a very remote area, a sat phone is the most reliable choice of communications device.

> **SURVIVAL FACTOID**
>
> Research found that lost and stranded victims typically became lost late in the day, an hour or two before nightfall.

243 Do Not Get Lost

If you are hiking in unknown territory, you should:

- Carefully follow the blazes or cairns to stay on the trail
- Bring a map and a compass
- Make note of landmarks when you go off-trail to see sights or answer the call of nature

244 Pause at the Intersections

Any juncture in the trail is an opportunity to get lost. Each time you come to a fork or Y in the path, pause. Orient yourself to make sure you know where you are going. Turn around and look back the way you came so you will recognize it again.

Identify Landmarks

245

Take note of any remarkable features of the landscape that could help you identify where you are, such as unusually shaped rocks or downed trees or stumps.

Use the Buddy System

246

If you have to go off trail, one person should stay on the trail, and keep eyes on you for as long as possible.

Admit When You Are Lost

247

As soon as you realize you have wandered off the trail and cannot see any blazes or trail indicators, stop. If you become at all disoriented, you will only it worse by continuing to travel. Just stop, and take a breath. Never be embarrassed or afraid to admit you don't know where you are.

Remember to STOP

248

S = Sit
T = Think
O = Observe
P = Plan

> "There is no bad weather, only bad clothing."
> —Swedish Saying

As soon as you realize you're in trouble, your nervous system will go into overdrive and panic is likely to set in. You need to STOP and arrest this process if you are going to survive. Sit: If you can, literally sit down. If you cannot sit, then stop moving, hold yourself still, and take a deep breath. Keep breathing until panic lifts and you begin to feel calm. **Think:** Now that your fight-or-flee response has been tamped down, you can use the cognitive part of your brain. Your first thought is to admit you are in trouble, and commit to tackling your situation with a calm, positive attitude. **Observe:** Assess your situation. Do not rush this step. Evaluate the full extent of your situation, asking yourself the following questions: Am I safe—what are the immediate dangers? Where am I—when was the last time you knew your location for sure? What do I need to do to survive? What are my resources? **Plan:** Based on your answers to the previous questions, you need come up with possible plans, evaluate them, and choose a course of action.

249 Know Your Priorities

The 3 top needs if you are lost in the wilderness: shelter, fire, and water. With a sturdy lean-to or A-frame shelter, a good fire, and a supply of drinking water, you are set up to survive for a very long time. Then you can focus on making yourself visible and easy to find. There are scenarios whereby the order of the game plan changes. For example, if you are lost in the heat of summer or stranded in the desert, finding or making drinkable water might become your number one task. Or if you realize you are lost in an area that is unsafe due to topography or critters, moving out might be the best decision. That's where the "think" part of STOP comes in!

250 If You Are Lost, Stay Put

Many people react to realizing that they are lost by panicking and attempting to find their own way out, which usually ends poorly. Staying put is almost always the better idea. Especially if your outdoor navigation and survival skills are minimal, your chances of finding your own way out very low—instead, your goal should be rescue. Staying put dramatically increases your chances of being found by searchers. It also gives you a chance to take care of injuries as well as basic needs like shelter and warmth, and helps you avoid exhaustion and further injuries.

Keep Busy (But Don't Waste Calories)

251

A busy person stays focused, alert, and positive, taking sensible actions to promote survival, instead of feeling depressed and hopeless. However, do not waste calories on unnecessary tasks. For example, feed long pieces of firewood into the campfire, rather than spending time and energy cutting up wood into small pieces. If you forage for food, make certain that the calories gathered exceed the calories spent gathering. It is also important to rest and sleep when possible.

Do Not Fear Starvation

252

Most healthy individuals can survive for weeks with little or no food. The length of time depends on many factors, including one's personal body fat percentage, metabolism, health factors, and weather conditions, but there are many accounts of individuals surviving for months without food. Rarely does the coroner's report in a case of a lost person's death list starvation as the cause. So as you are planning your survival strategy, do not allow low food stores to make you panic. See tip xx for finding food in the wilderness.

> *It's not the mountains that will stop you, it's the grain of sand in your shoe.*"

Calculate Your Water Needs

253

Water is the thing you cannot survive without. Depending on the weather conditions, and environment you are stuck in, you can typically survive for no more than about 3 days without water. In the heat of the desert, that period can drop to mere hours. The general rule for water needs: If the temperature if approximately 68°F (20°C), the average adult in conditions of normal exertion loses and therefore requires half to three-quarters of an ounce of water per pound (30 to 45 mL per kg) per day. Hot or cold temperatures, altitude, activity levels, or injury/illness will increase your need for water.

254 Assess Your Water Supply

If you planned your trip properly and have not lost your gear, you will have water supplies with you and water purification equipment on you. Determine how long your supplies can last before you need to seek out a source of water. See tips # tk to tk for finding and purifying water.

255 Maintain Your Body Temperature

Hypothermia or heat exhaustion/heat stroke can happen in minutes or hours, or slowly over days. Maintaining your body temperature in the healthy range is essential to survival. That's why proper survival clothing and footwear, constructing a shelter, and building a fire are the critical steps to surviving in the wilderness.

256 Prepare to Be Rescued

Studies also show that lost people, addled by panic and sleep deprivation, doom themselves by failing to plan to be rescued. Instead they make bad choices, including: sleeping during the day, making it difficult for search and rescue parties to find them; and making no attempts at building a fire or shelter, or signaling for help. As a result, when found they are often exhausted, hypothermic, dehydrated, and/or injured.

SURVIVAL FACTOID

Up to 50% of all search and rescues are false alarms. Increasingly, people who required rescue due to poor planning or foolish behavior are being held accountable, either through fines or charges such as "failure to carry the necessities of life" or by being billed for the cost of the SAR.

Know How Search and Rescue Works

A search is usually triggered by a distress call and/or occurrence report. If SAR is engaged, some combination of the following actions well ensure: SAR officials will check with family and friends, identify and profile the victim(s), establish the last-seen location, and taking into account the topography, weather, and season, use modeling software to help develop a search plan. They may use ATV or offroad vehicles, snowmobiles, boats, ground search teams, canine teams, aircraft, drones, park rangers, local and regional police, military personnel, and volunteers. SAR costs may range from $30,000 to $250,000 per day, per person. Searches typically continue until victims are found. Many wilderness parks are now requiring adventurers to show proof of skills and making it mandatory to bring survival gear and communications devices on any excursion.

SURVIVAL FACTOID

Studies show that approximately 99% of lost persons are found within 24 to 72 hours. After 4 to 6 days lost, the odds of being found alive decrease to approximately 75%, and after 7 days, outcomes are much less optimistic.

Make Yourself Easy to Find

- Stay put
- Build a large fire
- Wear bright colors
- Use a signal device

Check the Weather

Smart hikers maintain a high level of awareness for potential severe weather not only before but also during their travels. A smart phone and cell phone amplifier can give you access to online weather reports and weather satellite/radar maps. A handheld GPS unit with a barometric altimeter gives you pressure drop warnings. A simple windup or solar am/fm radio can give you access to marine and weather reports. Assign someone on the outside to contact you in case severe warnings are issued.

260 Avoid a Thunderstorm

Thunderstorms can be, and often are, deadly. In addition to checking reputable weather reports frequently, be alert to signs of a potential storm:

- Tall cumulus clouds—if puffy white clouds are building into towering shapes, a storm is likely on its way
- Tall, dark anvil-shaped clouds with flat bottoms—these are thunderclouds. If you see them, find shelter fast

261 Descend Early

Mountain storms often come in the afternoon. During storm season or if there is any likelihood of a storm, experienced mountain hikers descend no later than 2pm to avoid being caught on an exposed summit or mountainside during a storm.

262 Be Alert to Nature's Weather Warnings

Observe and learn to recognize weather patterns. In some cases, old-fashioned weather lore can be useful: "Red sky at night, sailor's delight/Red sky in morning, sailors take warning." This is true in both the northern and southern hemispheres, from about 30 to 60 degrees latitude. A red sky at night indicates high pressure and likely clear weather, while a red sky in the morning suggests low pressure and a storm blowing in from the west.

Survival Story

During a canoe trip to a semi-remote wilderness, after a half-day paddle in from the main highway, a group decided to camp on a scenic small island. When a severe thunderstorm struck the area, a live tree fell directly on a tent with 2 campers. One of the campers had severe internal injuries. The leader of the group saved the victim's life by stabilizing the tree, tenting a shelter all around her, and not moving her until medics arrived.

Researchers discovered that lost victims usually react to their situation with feelings of panic and embarrassment, and often attempt to find their own way out to avoid further embarrassment. SAR typically finds lost persons just a few miles from where they became lost, although they might have walked as much as 50 to 100 miles (80 to 160 km), usually in circles and often downhill, while trying to find their own way out.

Learn Weather Patterns

263

Understanding tidal movements, being able to recognize the meanings of different cloud shapes and patterns, understanding barometric pressure readings, and having a basic understanding of wind patterns will help you immeasurably in enjoying your outdoor activities and avoiding disaster.

Use the Flash-to-bang Method

264

To measure how close you are to an impending thunderstorm, count the number of seconds between the light flash and the loud bang. Divide by 5 to get the number of miles and by 3 to get the number of kilometres.) If there is less than a 30-second delay from flash to bang, then you are in danger. Be sure to allow time to get to safety before the time between lightning and its thunder reaches 30 seconds. Stay in the safe location for 30 minutes or more after the last thunder heard.

Seek Low Ground

265

The safest place to be if you're caught outside during a storm is the lowest place. If you're on the mountain, find the lowest spot possible, and if you see a ditch or depression, get in it if you can. Stay away from metal fences, power lines, bridges, railway tracks, and the like. Do not get caught on the water, and get as far inland from the shore as you can before the storm hits.

Survive a Thunderstorm

266

If your preventive measures have failed and you are caught

in backcountry during a thunderstorm, lightning is the main worry. Avoid open areas such as meadows or lakes, and high points such as summits and ridges. Get to a lower elevation as fast you can before the lightning starts.

- Toss away metal objects (tent poles, hiking gear) and don't use your cell phone
- Stay away from isolated trees and other tall objects (tall objects attract lightning)
- A heavily treed area is safe, but don't stand under the tallest tree
- Companions should space out at least 20 feet (6 m) from each other
- If you are near your vehicle, get in and close the windows—don't touch the metal
- Don't shelter in your tent
- If you cannot find shelter, crouch into a low ball with feet close together
- Do not lie down; ground current can run through you

267 Practice Your Lightning Crouch

The safest position to take if you are exposed in a storm is the lightning crouch. The goal is to make yourself an unattractive target for electrical current by getting low and minimizing your contact with the ground. Hunker down into a tight ball, keeping your head low, and balance on the balls of your feet, heels together. Put your hands over your ears.

268 Understand the Need for Shelter

Survival in the wilderness requires looking after your most important physical and psychological needs. A shelter is critical not only to maintaining warmth or staying out of the sun, but also for security. Survival shelters should be as small as is possible (easier to build, requiring less material, and faster to construct.)

Know What Makes a Good Shelter

269

A good shelter prevents heat loss by conduction (heat being sucked out of you by the cold ground) and convection (wind, cold air, and wetness preventing you from retaining warmth.) A good short-term survival shelter has thick flooring/bedding, a pitched roof with thick roofing materials, can accommodate a fire nearby or inside, and is small and completely sealable. You can find a shelter, adapt the natural features around into a shelter, or construct one. The easiest shelter designs are the A-frame and lean-to.

Scout a Good Shelter Location

270

A good site selection can be as or more important than the shelter itself. Follow the same rules as you would for choosing a camping site.

Pick a Dry Location

271

- Avoid small islands, peninsulas, and spits of land that could flood
- Always opt for higher ground: no ravines, narrow valleys, or ditches
- Avoid low-lying areas and dried stream beds that could fill in a storm
- Stay at least 200 ft (60 m) from water's edge

SURVIVAL FACTOID

Ground current causes approximately 50% of lightning injuries.

Find a Rock

272

Rock outcroppings are great to lean poles up against for a shelter, and they afford you a reflective radiating fireplace as well.

Site for Comfort and Safety

273

- Pick a flat area
- In hot conditions, choose a shaded spot
- In cool conditions, pick a sunny spot

- If wind is an issue, look for a windbreak to shelter your site
- Avoid obvious dangers such as insect nests, animal dens, and dead trees
- Look up and make sure there is nothing obvious that can fall on you, such as dead branches or large nuts

274 **Locate Your Shelter Near Necessities**

Choose a location with:

- Access to firewood suppl and drinking water source
- Proximity to an open area for118 HOW TO START A FIRE WITH WATER SURVIVE IN THE visibility and signaling

275 **Bivouac Sack or Tent + Sleeping Bag = Shelter**

If you have your bivy sack or tent and sleeping bag, you have an easy and efficient (though minimal) survival shelter already. Unless you also have a foam underpad, you should gather some insulating materials such as leaves, pine needles, and soft boughs for underneath.

276 **Use a Cave or Rock Outcropping**

Caves or rocky outcroppings can offer advantages in survival situations. There are real dangers, however, including instability of the rock that may lead to collapse, and the possibility of encountering other creatures such as bears, foxes, snakes, scorpions, or bats that may be already using that cave. If you spot a likely cave structure that you think might make a good shelter, first carefully scope it out for signs of animal use including tracks, hair/fur, bones, and spoor. If you are reasonably certain it is not in use, press hard all around the rock edges to make sure it seems stable and there are no loose or crumbling parts. Add insulating materials to the floor area, and block off the entrance, if possible, with a tarp or debris. If it is safe to do so, make your fire nearby.

Adapt a Boat to Give Shelter

277

If you have a canoe, fishing boat, or other small vessel, you can quickly and easily make a shelter from it, just like the historic Voyageurs (Canadian fur traders who paddled canoes on long wilderness journeys.) Gather rocks, strong branches with (forked) Y-shaped ends, or debris and use them to prop up the bow and stern of your boat on a 45-degree angle. Drape a tarp over the exposed side, and place some insulation/bedding inside. If the boat is made of metal such as aluminum, you can safely have a fire partially underneath or very close at hand.

Find Shelter Under an Evergreen

278

In an emergency survival scenario where you have limited time in severe conditions, look for a tall, thickly boughed evergreen such as a spruce, pine, or balsam tree, with branches that sweep low to the ground and some open space around the trunk. Clear out large hunks of debris and use the space beneath the branches as an impromptu shelter. It will provide some protection from the elements, and is better than being out in the open.

Turn a Garbage Bag into Sleeping Bag

279

If you have nothing but a large, strong garbage bag, you can still create a safe, warm place to sleep: fill the bag with soft, dry leaves, grasses, cattails or other fluffy natural materials, such as milkweed fluff.

Gather Materials to Build a Shelter

280

Gathering materials is faster than cutting or sawing down. Good choices for building a shelter include:

- evergreen boughs
- tree branches of all thicknesses, some with forked branches
- saplings, some with forked branches
- large, punky logs

- leaves
- grasses, cattails, large-leafed plants (that are nontoxic, if possible)
- birchbark and other large pieces of dead bark
- large flat rocks
- any gear that you might have retained, such as tarps, space blankets, rope, duct tape

> " *Think like a beaver when building a shelter: The more bedding and roofing, the better!* "

Use garbage bags or a tarp to gather large amounts of building supplies quickly. You can tie up loads of branches and bark, and drag them back to your building site.

281 Prioritize Activities

If it is late in the day with minimal light left, gather your materials to your building site, then get a fire going, before building into the night. If a storm is coming, get a shelter up before making a fire.

282 Break a Long Branch

Find two trees close together, place the branch horizontally across the trees, and pull it towards yourself.

283 Face a Shelter Opening to the Southeast

Often, a southeast-facing opening will shield you from most wind or rainstorms. If you know your weather is coming from another direction, act accordingly.

284 Build an A-Frame Shelter

An A-frame is a very easy and secure type of shelter that you can assemble quickly. Choose a location (a healthy tree with a low branch can serve as a support for your ridgepole.) Gather 2 sturdy, forked branches (with a Y-shape at the end and a longer tail), a sturdy branch as long as you are tall to serve as a ridgepole, a multitude of other branches (ideally with forks), and some leaves, boughs, pine needles and other bedding materials.

1. Wedge the forked sticks into an A-shape, then wedge or lash the ridgepole into the junction of the A, leading down to the ground on an angle.
2. Place a layer of bedding materials inside on the "floor."
3. Lean the extra branches up against the lodge pole on an angle, like "ribs."
4. If you have a tarp or space blanket, lay it over the structure and use rocks to hold it down. Otherwise, apply the smaller branches to the sides of your shelter to fill in the spaces, and layer your insulating materials thickly—you want at least 1 foot (30 cm)—on top and all around to keep out wind, rain, or snow).
5. Once inside, use remaining insulation materials to block off the entrance.

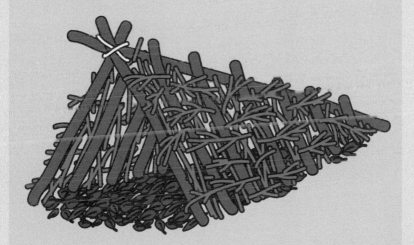

Construct a Lean-to Shelter

285

A lean-to is another extremely simple shelter consisting of a pole or rope used as a cross beam between 2 trees or poles, and branches or a tarp leaning up against it. The lean-to provides reasonable shelter in fine weather but it does not keep out rain, snow, or wind. You will need to gather a sturdy branch to act as your ridgepole or crossbeam.

1. Find 2 trees (ideally with forked branches that can be used to hold the lean-to pole) OR cut two strong branches into poles, each with one end carved to a point that can be staked into the ground.
2. If you have strong rope such as paracord, lash it to the trees so it creates a support over which to drape your tarp or space blanket.
3. If you are using a wood cross-pole, place your crossbeam into the forks or lash it to the trees/support poles.
4. If you have a tarp or blanket (or even a rain poncho), drape it over the cross-pole and tie the top edges to the pole and the bottom to the ground with rocks.
5. If you are using branches as your wind-break instead of a tarp, lean them up against the crossbeam in a tight formation to form a strong frame.
6. In windy conditions, thickly layered branches will help to provide support to prevent a tarp from being blown off or shredded.

Make a Tarp Shelter

If all you have is a piece of plastic—a garbage bag, space blanket, or tarp, for example, and a hiking pole, you can create a very simple shelter. Wedge or hammer your pole into the ground, then drape your plastic over it, securing the edges/sides to saplings and rocks. Another option, if you have rope or cord, is to tie one end to a strong, overhanging branch of a healthy tree and the other end to the center of your tarp, to create a kind of hanging tipi. Use rocks to secure the bottom to the ground.

Learn to Build an Advanced Shelter

If you are an experienced adventurer trekking to extremely remote places or in extreme weather conditions, you should know how to build advanced shelters such as quinzhee snow huts, igloos, raised jungle shelters, and other long-term, harsh environment shelters. These require specialized knowledge and often equipment, as well. You would do well to take a course from a reputable, experienced expert, and have built practice shelters before you go on your next adventure.

Protect Yourself from Sun and Heat in the Desert

If you are trekking in desert locations, your shelter needs will be different. In the extreme heat of daytime, you need protection from the sun and heat. See tip XX for appropriate clothing. Even with a hat, you may need to shelter yourself while walking. Create mobile shade by using an umbrella.

289 Build a Desert Shelter

If conditions are so hot during that day that you need to shelter from the sun and not exert yourself, build this shelter in the very early morning hours before the sun is up. Choose a location between dunes for protection from wind but not in a low-lying area where flooding could wipe out your shelter and put you at risk. Look for rock outcroppings, boulders, or ledges to provide support. As always, avoid places where you can see evidence of animals or snakes. You will need 8 sticks or stakes that you can plant in the ground. Working slowly to avoid overheating

- Dig a space deep enough for you to lie down
- Pile the dirt or sand dug from the trench around outer edges to build up the sides of the trench
- Plant a stake at each of the four corners of the trench
- Tie a corner of your darkest covering (tarp, sheet, blanket) to each stake, so that it forms a flat roof over the trench with enough space for you to lie beneath
- Using four taller stakes and a white sheet (for reflecting sunlight) or a space blanket, hang a second flat roof a few inches above the first flat roof.

If you have rope but not stakes, build a tarp-style shelter (see tip xx.) Tie a brightly colored piece of clothing to one stake to alert searchers to your presence.

290 Move at Night in the Desert

If you must travel rather than stay put, but is too hot to travel in the daytime, take advantage of the lower temperatures of desert nights to travel.

291 Protect Yourself from Sand

To protect yourself from heavily blowing sand, wear

goggles, and wrap cloth around your ears, nose, and mouth. If you cannot find shelter, mark the direction of your travel, then lie down flat to wait out the storm.

Build a Platform Shelter

If you are lost in a region where the ground is wet, such as the jungle, you will need a raised shelter so you can stay dry. A raised shelter is also useful in places where insects or snakes are plentiful. You will need 4 long posts or stakes, 2 cross pieces, and a number of longer branches.

- Drive the posts into the ground
- Lash the supporting cross pieces to the posts
- Lay branches lengthwise to create a platform
- Place a foam pad if you have it or leaves or other debris on top of the platform to create cushioning and insulation

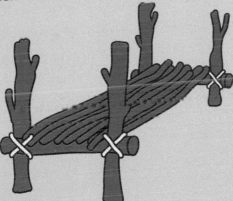

Bamboo is probably the most useful and versatile single plant in the world. Not only can it serve for any part of your shelter, but it also contains clean drinking water in its hollow segments, can be used as boat pontoons with the air in its hollow segments, makes a great drinking straw and blow gun, flexible fishing pole, canteen, hammock, and more.

Create a Hammock from a Tarp

Any strong fabric will do. You will need at least 20 feet (6 m) of strong nylon rope.

- Roll the long sides of the tarp towards the middle until it looks like 2 long tubes.
- Fold over one end of the bundled tarp into a J-shape. Wrap the rope around the J at least 2 times, then pass the rope under itself (a double sheet bend), pulling it tight. Repeat on the other end.
- Wrap the ends of the rope at least twice around 2 trees about 10 feet (3 m) apart, as high as you can reach.

Now you have a hammock protected from the ground. To further protect yourself from things that might drop from the trees, use another rope to string up an A-frame tarp over your hammock.

294 Repel Insects from Your Shelter

If you have any DEET-based insect repellant, spray it on your ropes and outside of your hammock or tarp.

295 Tie a Clove Hitch

The clove hitch is a simple basic knot that everyone should know.

296 Lash Sticks Together

Being able to lash sticks or branches together is a crucial outdoor skill. Practice before you go—learning while night descends or rain drenches you is not going to be fun!

1. Cross two branches are poles to be perpendicular.
2. Make a clove hitch knot on the vertical branch near the crossing point.
3. Weave the rope under and over the crossed sticks

alternately, first over the horizontal bar, around behind the vertical bar, then back over the front of the horizontal bar on the left. Tighten.

4. Bring the rope behind the vertical bar and up the right front side of the horizontal bar; repeat four times.

5. Use "frapping" to wrap the rope between the branches, weaving the cord in front of the back one and in back of the front one several times. Pull it tight.

6. One last clove hitch will securely fasten the two branches to each other.

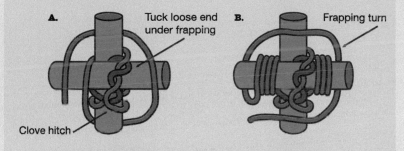

A. Tuck loose end under frapping

Clove hitch

B. Frapping turn

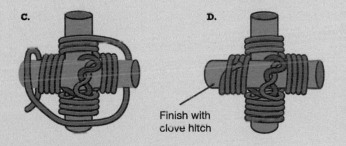

C.

D. Finish with clove hitch

Practice Starting a Fire Before You Go

297

Never go into the wilds without having successfully practiced starting and maintaining a fire multiple times.

Bring Multiple Fire-starting Tools on Every Trip

298

Fire provides warmth purifies water, signals for help, cooks food, raises spirits, keeps wildlife at bay, and smokes out insects! Survival experts and survivors themselves agree that fire is one of the most important priorities in a short-term survival situation. For this reason, you should always bring at least 2 and better, 3 fire-starting methods along anytime you head into the wilderness. My preferences:

- waterproof matches
- at least one and preferably several butane lighters
- a magnesium-flint rod

299 Understand the Science of Fire

Oxygen, ignition, and fuel are the necessary components of any fire. Oxygen is readily available from the air. Fuel consists of tinder—the finest of flammable materials, such as dried grasses or cattail fluff; kindling—small dried twigs (I find the best are from evergreens), and fuel wood—any dry wood sticks, branches, or logs, thumb-sized and larger. Ignition is the spark that lights it up, provided by your matches, lighter, or flint rod. Fire occurs when an external igniter such as a spark or flame is applied to the fuel and heats the fuel and the oxygen, increasing molecular activity and creating a self-sustaining chemical reaction (after which the external ignition source is no longer required). A fire will continue until all the available fuel has been consumed, the fuel and/or oxygen is removed, or the temperature is reduced by cooling.

300 Design a Good Campfire

The most efficient design of a basic campfire is the teepee or cone style.

- Tinder goes at the bottom
- Layer kindling around the tinder in a circular pattern with the ends converging at the top
- Place fuel wood on top
- Keep materials loose and aerated.

SURVIVAL TIP

For a very efficient fire-starting fuel "bomb," gather a bundle of dried evergreen twigs, place pine needles and birch bark and fluffy materials inside, and have larger fuel wood branches ready!

Find Good Tinder

Tinder should be dry and Search around for good quantities of the following tinder:

- dried grasses or similar dried plant material
- dried pine needles
- fluffy plant materials such as milkweed puffs, dried goatsbeard, or cattails
- finely shredded birch bark
- an abandoned bird or mouse nest
- red oak leaves (their natural oils make them burn fast and well)
- dryer lint
- pine sap, spruce or balsam gum
- hair
- straw
- paper
- pieces of fleece clothing
- pine cones
- any dried twigs

Use a Fire Ring or Pit

A safe fire is a contained fire. Always create or use a pre-existing fire ring that is bordered with rocks or dig out a fire pit down to mineral or sandy soil. Clear all vegetation away from your fire site.

303 Bring Home-made Fire-Starters

Many items can be used as tinder, and most will work even better when soaked with alcohol-based hand sanitizer or petroleum jelly. Make these in advance and pack them in your kit:

- Cotton balls
- Steel wool
- Sanitary pads
- Dyer lint wrapped in wax paper
- Sawdust rolled in wax paper
- Duct tape (petroleum-based duct tape is highly flammable)
- Scraps of cotton toweling or clothing dipped in paraffin

304 Find Dry Fuel Wood

Dry (or "seasoned") wood comes from dead trees, which may be still standing or lying on the ground. Standing wood will have to be chopped down or branches broken off. If logs are already down, and the bark is gone or partially gone, the tree indicates that the tree is probably dry. If you can, gather standing wood over ground wood, since the standing pieces tend to be much drier and easier to light. Be sure to start gathering firewood as far away from your shelter site as is reasonable, leaving a nearby supply for later should you be there long enough to weaken. Note that abandoned beaver lodges and dams can provide a good supply of firewood. Tree stumps from a forest fire are great for getting a quick fire since the resin has been drawn

Survival Story

During a winter survival simulation for a television show, I once burned through an entire face cord of wood (a stack of firewood measuring 4 feet wide by 8 feet long, or 1.2 x 2.4 m.) I realized that feeding long branches into the fire saved me the time and effort of chopping the wood into smaller pieces and kept the fire hot and steady.

out due to the heat of the forest fireplaces.

Gather and Store Firewood Efficiently

305

Use a rope to tie a pile of dry branches together, and drag them back to your survival site. If you think that you have enough firewood for the night, go back and gather twice as much. Know that gathering enough for a few days ensures that you will be supplied in case of rain or snow. Always cover up your firewood supply with a tarp or pieces of bark.

Choose the Right Woods

306

Hardwoods are dense and therefore best for a hot, long-burning fire without too much smoking or sparking, and for providing warmth in the form of coals. Hardwoods typically have broad leaves, and lose them in the fall; examples include oak, maple, beech, elm, and ash. Softwoods are fast-growing conifers and evergreens, resinous and with needles. They are lighter and less dense, and therefore good for quickly flaming and burning hot and fast—great for kindling—but also smoky and sparky. They leave behind ash rather than coals. Typically, softer woods such as pine, cedar, and fir are found in the lower lying areas, whereas hardwoods are usually found farther from water.

Smoke Out Bugs

307

Rotting, punky logs are great for a smoky fire that deters insects.

Use Green Wood to Keep a Fire Smoldering

308

When you don't need a hot, high flame but want smoldering, in a signal fire, for example, use live wood.

Start a Fire Using an Evergreen Tree

309

Evergreen branch knots are filled with resin, which lights quickly. Use evergreen boughs that have visible knots for best results.

310 Build a Large Fire

Rather than trying to stack and build one large fire, instead construct and then connect several smaller fires.

311 Get a Spark by Shorting Out a Flashlight

Open a flashlight or headlamp with the batteries still in, and connect a thin piece of wire to both terminals. Add some fluffy, fine tinder material to the terminals, and upon getting a spark, remove tinder quickly to prevent damage to the flashlight.

312 Carry Waterproof Matches

Purchase specialized stormproof matches that will light in rain and wind. You can also buy strike-anywhere matches, and coat them in wax or paraffin, or keep them in a waterproof container. If you have a limited number of matches left, you could carefully slice a single match into as many as four matches!

313 Carry a Survival Lighter

These rugged butane fuel lighters can be refueled. Note that they can be dangerous to use due to intense flame.

314 Bring Flint and Magnesium Sticks

There are many brands and models of flint and magnesium rods on the market. My favorite have a blend of flint (selenium) and magnesium, which spark at a very high heat, so that when you strike the sparks into a tinder nest, the fire starts fast and strong. A separate flint rod and a magnesium block also work well, however, you first have to take a few minutes to scarpe the magnesium shavings into the tinder nest, and then hit a spark.

These work even when wet. The downside is that you have to know how to use them, and have good tinder materials.

Start a Fire with Steel Wool and Batteries

315

Simply connect superfine or extra-fine steel wool to the negative and positive ends of a battery. For batteries under 5 volts, use 2 batteries, connecting negative to positive. For a 9-volt, just touch the positive terminal with the steel wool. Don't buy coarse steel wool or soap pad steel wool, as they are difficult to use.

SURVIVAL FACTOID

The author has started a firebow fire in 5 seconds, an unofficial world record.

Use Potato Chips for Kindling

316

The worse the chips are for you (filled with saturated fats and oils), the better they burn as kindling. Corn chips and other junk food chips work, too.

Create Fire from Friction

317

Though this is possible, it's extremely difficult and is best left to the hobbyists! In our advanced survival camps, we teach how to start a fire with a firebow and hand drill. We spend a full day instructing, and maybe one out of ten participants becomes adept at achieving a fire. It can take hours or even days to gather the proper woods, carve it all up, and hope that the humidity in the air is low enough to be conducive to success. Perhaps a few dozen folks in North America are sufficiently expert to actually venture out into the wilds, gather up the materials, carve up the components, and get a fire going by this method. It is true that native peoples used this method, but they would keep a set of implements prepared, and more commonly they transported their fire, buried their fire, and kept their fire going at all times.

Start a Fire with Water

318

Yes, you can start a fire with water. Your water source can be a large ice cube, a plastic water bottle or plastic bag filled with water, even a sheet of plastic half-filled with water. You will need a clear day so the sun can provide your ignition—this method is unlikely to work on a cloudy day—and the best time to try it is at noon, with the sun overhead and at its hottest. You will also need tinder (see tip xx) and something to magnify the sun's rays, such as a magnifying glass, mirror or other reflective surface (such as a shiny spoon), or reading glasses.

- Direct the magnified concentrated rays into a tinder nest
- Be ready with your kindling to catch and spread the flame

319 Keep a Fire Going During Wet Weather

To keep your fire alight during rain or snowfall, you will need to build a roof over it, but if that is not possible, place large logs over the fire, since they will protect the fire and it should continue to smolder slowly.

320 Practice Fire Safety

Always practice fire safety:

- Select an open spot away from trees, logs, overhanging branches, and stumps
- build your fire away from flammable grasses, vegetation, and dry brush
- construct fire away from windy areas
- always prepare a base of rock from flat stones, which will reflect heat and help prevent the fire spreading where you don't want it
- never build a fire on top of organic or forest floor soils
- build a firebreak or divider from rocks or green logs to separate bedding and shelter materials from the fire
- never leave a fire unattended; if necessary, bury the coals for later restart

> " ...when one learns to live off the land entirely, being lost is no longer life-threatening."
> —Dean Olsen

- watch your flammable hair and polyester clothing!
- Keep water or a shovel nearby for dousing flames

Put a Fire Out Safely

321

Drown the fire with plenty of water (a garbage bag filled with water makes a good fire bucket.) Mix ashes and embers with soil. Scrape partially burned sticks to be sure hot embers are down to ash. To ensure that your fire is out, dig around for hidden coals, and feel with your hands just to be safe; then soak an area at least a foot or two beyond the fire perimeter.

Heat Stones to Create Lasting Warmth in a Shelter

322

The pioneers used to heat up stones and bricks, and place them on a metal tray or pan under their beds for warmth through the cold nights. You can do the same thing by heating small, flat stones until they are hot to touch, and placing them in places where you have excessive heat loss (near feet, head, back). Make sure that the stones are not glowing, since they could cause an unwanted fire or burns. Also, never heat up rocks from a river, or rocks that are wet and saturated, or limestones as all of these have the potential to explode.

Transport a Fire

323

If you need to move your fire, use a fire bundle. Start by constructing a fire with hardwoods, and create a bed of coals. Next, make a fire-bundle nest by taking some punky, rotting wood that is semi-moist, and adding some cedar bark crushed inside, then wrap with birchbark or other leaves. Place coals in the center, and keep it a touch aerated. While transporting, blow slowly on it every so often to see if everything is still working, but not to hard as to create a lot of smoke and a flame. Use a tin can with a handle, or a hollowed out animal skull for easier transport.

324 Understand What Makes Water Safe for Drinking

Before you go looking for a source of water, it is important to understand when water is safe to drink. Imagine yourself on a mountain hike, coming across a beautiful flowing stream or a clear mountain lake. The environment is pristine. Should you drink the water? The answer is, probably not—or at least, not straight from the lake or stream. Bacteria (e.g., E. coli, salmonella), viruses (e.g., hepatitis A), protozoa (e.g., cryptosporidia and giardia), and other microscopic natural organisms occur in wetlands, lakes, rivers, ponds, and streams. You cannot see them—they may be present even in sparkling clear waters. Dead animals in the water upstream or a previous camper who bathed in your waters may have contaminated the water with pathogens. Still other seemingly clean water may have natural mineral deposits or have been polluted in ways that could render the water not only unfit to drink but even deadly. The moral of the story? The safest course is to purify all water before you drink it.

> ### SURVIVAL TIP
>
> If you don't have a cup or any vessel to hold the water, you can soak it up in a cloth. Without something to squeeze it into, you won't be able to purify or disinfect though, so this is a last resort.

325 Check the CDC Drinking Water Treatment Guidelines

The American Center for Disease Control has a very thorough safe water recommendations document that you can find at www.cdc.gov/healthywater. The 3 methods of purification are filtering, treating with chemicals (usually iodine or chlorine), and boiling.

326 Find a Safe Source of Water in the Woods

Knowing that you should avoid drinking water directly from nature, the best sources for safe water if you have no other choice are:

- Clear, flowing water such as in a natural spring
- Clear flowing water in a visibly unpolluted stream with origins and a path far from human settlements

Always filter this water before drinking, and purify if possible. Unfortunately, contaminants like dioxin and mercury cannot be purified using portable or conventional methods, so stay away from rivers, which are all-too-often polluted from chemical or manufacturing sources.

Catch Rainwater or Frozen Water

327

Good sources are:

- Rainwater collected from a clean tarp
- Fresh snow and most sources of ice (not from saltwater)
- Glacial water

Although water collected via these methods is technically safe to drink, again, purifying before drinking is the safest course of action.

Find Water in the Desert

328

In the desert, finding water takes precedence. You will want to reduce your activity to lower your water needs, which means shading yourself from the sun, not moving in the heat of the day, and when you do move, going slowly so as not to perspire. Where to look for water in an arid landscape?

- Go down: look for low-lying stream or river beds or channels
- Dig down: in the lowest area you can find, dig down till you reach the water table
- Seek greenery: if you see plants, you will likely find a source of water—you may need to dig for it
- Look for rocks: water is more likely to be found near rock features
- Watch for birds and animals: they need water, too. If

you can follow them (carefully), they may lead you to
water; dawn and dusk are the best times
- Collect it: Make a solar still (see tip # xx)

Purify all the water you find before drinking it.

329 **Get Water from Plant Vapors**

If you have plastic bags, you can try wrapping them
tightly around plants. After several hours, you may find
that the plant has released water through the process of
evapotranspiration. Be very careful if you must use this
method to choose a familiar plant, as a poisonous plant will
release poisonous water. If you need to test an unfamiliar
plant, follow the steps in tip #xx.

330 **Know Which Plants to Use**

The prickly pear (Opuntia) is a North American cactus
that is often touted as a source of moisture in the desert.
However, the fluid from this and most other cacti (especially
the barrel cacti) contains substances that can make you
sick. Drinking from cacti may at best lead to diarrhea, which
will make you even more dehydrated, and at worst, may
kill you. In Australia, water can be found at the base of
certain eucalyptus plants, but you would need to be able to
recognize them. Know before you go which plants are safe,
or avoid them.

331 **Catch the Morning Dew**

Before the sun has fully risen, you may be able to collect
dew that has formed on plants or rocks. You might set out
flat rocks at night to see if they
can amass enough dew to wet
your whistle.

332 **Dig for Water**

Whenever you dig for water, make
a narrow hole that goes down at

SURVIVAL TIP

Despite what you may have
heard, drinking your own
urine is not ideal. If you
must, try to distil or filter
it first.

least 12 inches (30 cm). If you find the soil at that level to be damp, widen the hole to 10 to 15 inches (25 to 38 cm). Wait for water to collect at the bottom—note that this could take hours. Use the time to dig more holes.

Collect Water with a Tarp 333

Set up one or more tarps on an angle, and use them to funnel dew and rainwater into a tin can or container. Purify or filter before drinking.

Make a Solar Still 334

Dig a hole in nearby soil or sand. (A large bin or water container can also work if you're shipwrecked or stranded on a boat or raft.) Fill the hole with vegetation (salt water if on a boat.) Place a tin can in the center (or another vessel to catch the purified water). Place a clear plastic sheet over the hole, secure it with rocks or wood all around to prevent moisture escaping, and place a stone in the center of the plastic sheet to form a cone pointing downwards towards the tin can. The sun's heat will cause moisture to evaporate under the plastic cover, and water will roll down (due to gravity) into the tin can. Salt and other toxins will not evaporate.

Filter First 335

Though you cannot see bacteria and other microscopic contaminants, you can see all kinds of other stuff in water that you find or collect in nature, which is why it is a good idea to manually filter your water before boiling or treating it. Coffee filters are ideal for catching particles, but a t-shirt or other piece of clean cloth will suffice if you haven't got anything else.

Let It Stand 336

If you have nothing to filter water through, let it stand in a container for 12 hours, and particles will sink to the bottom. Purify before drinking.

337 Purify Water by Boiling

Boiling water kills pathogens. To create safe drinking water, simply boil it and cool to the desired temperature for drinking. Experts recommend keeping the water at a rolling boil for 3 minutes. If you cannot manage that, you may be okay anyhow, as water that reaches the point of pasteurization (158oF or 70 oC) is hot enough to kill pathogens. Water boils at 212oF (100 oC) at sea level and at a lower temperature at higher altitudes. So, at 10,000 feet above sea level, water boils at 194oF (90 oC), which is still higher than is necessary to purify water. If you can, however, boil for at least 3 minutes.

> *Adapt or perish, now as ever, is nature's inexorable imperative.''*
> —H. G. Wells

338 Add Boiling Time at Altitude

Though you should technically be safe with simply bringing the water to a boil, many experts prefer to use this general rule of thumb: bring water to a rolling boil for 3 minutes, at 1,000 to 5,000 feet (305 to 1,524 m) above sea level, and for additional 1,000 feet (305 m) of altitude, add another minute of boiling to be safe. At very high altitudes, boiling isn't recommended.

339 Disinfect Water Using Chlorine

Chlorine is widely available at most camping stores and water refill suppliers. It's reasonably tasteless compared to iodine, and is 99.9% effective against natural contaminants, but not totally reliable against viruses.

340 Use Household Bleach to Disinfect Water

Household bleach (that is, unscented chlorine bleach) can be used in a pinch. Add 1/8 teaspoon (.6 mL, or 8 drops) of regular, unscented, liquid household bleach for each gallon of water, stir or shake thoroughly, and let stand for 30 minutes before you use it. Store disinfected water in clean containers with covers.

Purify Water with Iodine

341

Iodine is widely agreed upon to be the most effect at water treatment, and is readily available at outdoor stores and medical retailers.

- Tincture of iodine 2%: To clear water, add 5 drops per quart (120 mL); double this for cloudy water. Cover, shake, and wait at least 30 minutes.
- Iodine drops or tablets: follow the manufacturer's instructions carefully.

Iodine has an aftertaste, which can be somewhat neutralized with flavor crystals, vitamin C, or even orange juice. Note that some people are allergic to iodine, and it should be used with caution by pregnant women, people with thyroid conditions, and those taking lithium, among others—check with your doctor and be sure others in your party have checked with their own physicians before relying on iodine for water purification.

Purify Water with Carbon or Ceramic Depth Filters

342

There are a variety of excellent water filter pumps and gravity-style filters that employ a ceramic or carbon medium to remove particles and purify water. Most of the toxins found in nature cannot make it through the very fine filtration found in these systems; however, it's still critically important to pre-filter prior to using one of these filtering systems. If you don't pre-filter, you risk clogging up the internal filter's guts, and worse, allowing some contaminants through. Beware filter systems that aren't fine enough to stop most toxins from getting through, since some are just good enough to improve taste, not toxicity.

Purify with Ultraviolet Filters

343

UV filters, which use ultraviolet light to purify the water, can be very effective. Portable camping UV filters such as the SteriPen are newer to the marketplace.

344 In Hot Weather, Boil at Night

For summer and warm weather or climate conditions, boil water at night, and leave it to cool down for use the next day.

345 Bring Multiple Methods of Reaching Help

Do not go on any outdoor trek without at least 2 of the following, and preferably one of the first two items:

- Personal locator beacon (PLB)
- Reliable communications equipment and back-up power for it
- Handheld flares (which can double as fire-starters)
- Signal mirror
- Glowsticks
- Laser pointers
- Brightly colored clothing items, surveying tape, or flags
- Whistle

> **SURVIVAL TIP**
>
> Site your signal fire in an open area, but do not choose a dry, brush-filled area where your fire could quickly burn out of control. Be cautious—a forest fire will not help you!

346 Know How to Signal for Help

An important survival skill is the ability to signal for assistance. If you brought adequate communications equipment and have been able to hang onto it, you should be able to reach SAR and get help swiftly. If not, you'll need to resort to more old-fashioned methods. Please practice before you go. With primitive signaling methods, the goal is to attract attention by being visible or noisy in ways that are noticeably different and stand out from the normal sights and sounds of the environment. Be opportunistic about signaling for help—that is, take every opportunity!

> **SURVIVAL TIP**
>
> Always check expiry dates of flares before buying or using. Once expired, they become volatile and could seriously backfire and injure you.

Learn the International Signals for Help

- SOS
- HELP
- MAYDAY-MAYDAY-MAYDAY
- 3 loud blasts on a whistle
- Any repeated pattern of 3s

Know Ground-to-Air Emergency Codes

If SAR is looking for you from above, you can use the international ground-to-air code to signal them about your condition or location. Form the shapes as large as you can in an open area. Branches, boughs, rocks, clothing, or debris can be formed into shapes; alternatively, use a large stick to scrape or dig the shapes into the earth.

- **V** Require assistance
- **X** Require medical assistance
- **N** No
- **Y** Yes
- → Proceed in this direction

Make a Signal Fire

Smoke is an excellent way to let SAR know where you are. A fire designed to attract help, unlike a survival fire, needs to be very smoky and visible. Choose a location near (ideally visible from) your camp, in a spot that is high and open. Clear the area of debris. Assemble plenty of tinder and fuel wood, plus a number of green (live) branches and boughs. Build your fire as in tip # xx. Once your fire is burning strongly, make it smoky by adding green wood or evergreen boughs. You can also prepare your fire, then build "walls" around it from the green material. Be ready to add

SURVIVAL TIP

During the daytime, dark smoke is more visible than white smoke. To make your signal smoke dark, pile on leafy green boughs, or an additive such as oil or any other petroleum product, or tires from an ATV or other vehicle.

fuel regularly to keep the fire burning, and continue to add green wood to keep it smoky.

350 Build a Triple Signal Fire

If you have space and materials, create a triple fire by making 3 small fires in a pyramidal or triangular shape, or in a row.

351 Use Saplings to Make Smoke

If you can find 3 or 4 green saplings relatively close together, you can use them to make a smoky fire. Create a "tripod" from by tying or weaving the saplings' tops together, and and stuff the interior area with flammable materials, such as evergreen boughs, foliage, birchbark, red oak leaves, dried grasses, sage brushes, or anything dry. If you can improvise a shelf to hold your tinder, even better.

352 Signal with a Mirror

A signal mirror (a small mirror with a hole in the middle) or a cosmetic mirror can be used to create a signal by flashing the sun's reflections in a pattern toward a target. If you have a vehicle, you can break off a rear view or side mirror; if you have DVDs in the vehicle, those (or any other reflective surface, including a knife blade, space blanket, or piece of foil) could also be used. You need a target for this signal to aim at—a rescue plane or a SAR crew, for example. Signal mirrors have instructions printed right on them. To aim other reflectors, move your mirror in one hand to get a reflection from the sun. Locate the reflected spot and bring up your other hand to "catch" it. Form a V-shape with your fingers and sight the spot through the V. Move the V and the reflection to your target. Wiggle the mirror

Survival Story

I have lost as much as 50 pounds in nine days of extreme survival in the Boreal forests. When I left, I was hungry but alive and well.

back and forth in a pattern of 3s to create a distress signal. Never aim the signal at a person's face or anyone close by.

Improvise a Visual Signal

353

If there is an open space such as a clearing or hilltop, or in winter, a frozen lake, you can set up visual SOS. Use clothing items, logs, piles of debris, or any other items you can find to "write" SOS or HELP, or any combination of 3 dashes or dots (i.e., 3 even piles of branches) will alert searchers to your presence.

Improvise an Audible Distress Signal

354

Sound can also effectively signal that you need help. Devices that can produce sound that will travel include whistles, air horns, and even banging on a metal plate or bottle. In order to create a recognizable distress signal, make your sound in a pattern of 3s, such as 3 short whistle blasts, followed by a 3-second pause, then 3 long whistle blasts. Repeat.

Signal with a Glowstick

355

Glowsticks offer several ways to attract attention at night. They can be seen from far away. Find a relatively open area, and try these methods:

- Arrange bright red or orange glowsticks to say SOS or in a 3s pattern
- Tie a string to one, and swing it around repeatedly 3 times, pausing in between repetitions.

Look for Food

356

While lack of food can cause discomfort, increase your risk of hypothermia, and lead to overall weakness, most healthy people can survive for several days or even weeks with little or no food. However, once you have shelter, fire, and water (and have signaled for help) it's time to think about eating. (Of course, before you went on this trip, you researched the local flora and fauna, so you have an idea already of what's available. Right?) Foraging for plant material, fishing, and hunting/trapping animals are the main sources of food in the wilderness.

357 Forage with Calories in Mind

The calories that you gather should far outweigh the cost of gathering the calories.

358 Put Safety First

Survival foraging is much more dangerous than foraging for fun or hobby. On an empty stomach and with compromised health, ingesting even something slightly toxic could in fact kill you. A wilderness survival situation is not the time to experiment with unknown plants or critters. Therefore the rule is Unless you are 100% certain that the plant or critter is edible, don't eat it!

359 Know the Signs

Signs that an unknown plant may be inedible or poisonous:

- Milky or discolored sap
- Spines, fine hairs, or thorns
- Beans, bulbs, or seeds inside pods
- Bitter or soapy taste
- Any odor of almonds stems and leaves
- Grain heads with pink, purplish, or black spurs
- Shiny leaves
- White and/or yellow berries
- Groups of 3 leaves (like poison ivy)

SURVIVAL FACTOID

Prior to the agricultural evolution, foraging and gathering was always essential to most human diets around the world, and for some peoples even today foraging remains a main source of food. Historically, foraging provided more stability than hunting and trapping.

Some plants with these characteristics may indeed be edible, but it's better to be safe than sorry. See tip # xx above. Also, do not eat rotting or moldy vegetation.

Never Eat Mushrooms

Even if you are an expert, never eat wild mushrooms in a survival situation. If you're wrong, you're dead.

Sample Safely: Separate, Contact, Taste

If you have no choice but to test a plant, follow this method:

Separate the plant into roots, stems, leaves, buds, and flowers. Examine all parts, and discard if you find worms or bugs. Crush the plant part and rub it on your skin, then wait at least 6 hours for a reaction. If contact with your skin causes a rash or irritation, this plant is probably not going to make your stomach feel good, either. Next, touch the plant part to your lip. If there is no unpleasant sensation such as tingling or burning, place it on your tongue—but do not chew and swallow. Let it sit for 15 minutes. If you do get a reaction, spit it out and rinse with water. Still no bad reaction? Chew. Wait another 10 minutes. If all is well, you can swallow. If 8 hours pass and all is still well, you have found a food (a plant part, this is) that you can eat.

Study Edible Plants

The forests, jungles, and even deserts of the Earth contain edible plants too numerous to mention. Before you venture into any environment, take the time to familiarize yourself with the local edible plants. A good field guide is invaluable, and if a pocket-sized version fits in your pack, so much the better.

Get Vitamins from Evergreens

Among the vast store of plant information that it would benefit you to know, here are a few facts about woodland plants to get you started:

- evergreen foliage is high in vitamin C
- pine cones yield pine nuts

- rose petals and rosehips are also high in vitamin C
- cattails are fully edible, the best parts are the lower stem, green pod, yellow pollen
- fiddleheads (young ferns) are a staple of haute local cuisine
- wild asparagus makes a delicious woodland salad
- dandelions are a powerfood, high in vitamins A, C, E and B-complex, plus iron
- rock tripe lichen (Umbilicaria) is high in protein
- acorns can be boiled and roasted, then pounded into powdery flour substitute
- many wild nuts yield edible oils, including beech, witch hazel, hickory, and walnuts
- maple, birch and sycamore trees all have edible sap

364 Eat Seaweed

If you are stranded near saltwater, you may be able to forage for edible seaweed, a veritable nutritional powerhouse, high in vitamins and minerals. Do not eat seaweed that has washed up on shore, as it may be rotting. Avoid eating seaweed near industrial or heavily populated shorelines. Many experts offer courses in seaweed foraging so you can learn precisely which types of this algae are best to eat. Never eat freshwater seaweed or algae.

365 Eat Bugs

Some examples of edible, though not necessarily tasty, critters include the following:

- Crickets
- Cicadas
- Crayfish
- Ants
- Worms
- Leeches
- Grasshoppers
- Snails
- Grubs

> " Generally speaking, a howling wilderness does not howl: it is the imagination of the traveler that does the howling."
> —Henry David Thoreau

Use a stick to dig under logs, rocks, and stumps. Grasshoppers may be easy to catch at dawn. Most insects are best eaten cooked, and then mashed up. Try wrapping them in leaves from plants you know are not toxic. Don't eat flies, mosquitoes, ticks, or bees and wasps (unless you remove the stinger.)

Hunt for Food

366

Creatures that are easy to catch using a stick, rock, or slingshot include porcupines, pheasants, frogs, snakes, turtles, and birds.

Use a Trap or Snare

367

With a trap or snare, many animals may be caught for food, including rabbits, squirrels, beavers, and many bird species. Snaring and trapping is a numbers game. Rather than setting up one or two fancy snares, try to setup dozens of simple snares, tied to branches or sapling bases. Good spots for snares include near water sources and wildlife throughways. A simple snare can be made from light to medium gauge brass wire, fishing line, dental floss, and even spruce roots. Make a small noose, and feed the wire through to form a fist-sized snare for small game (rabbits, groundhogs); double it for beavers and porcupines.

Make a Deadfall Trap

368

Deadfalls are baited traps to be placed near signs of wildlife. A simple deadfall uses sticks and bait to lure an animal; when it takes the bait, a heavy rock or log falls on the creature. To make a Figure 4 Deadfall, you will need 3 sturdy sticks of about the same length, a heavy

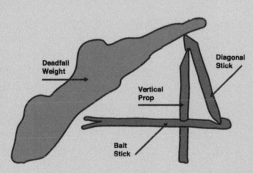

Deadfall Weight

Diagonal Stick

Vertical Prop

Bait Stick

rock or log, and a knife to cut notches, plus some bait. Ideally the trap stands on a hard surface or flat rock.

369 Fish for Food

If you are stranded near water, you may be able to catch fish for food. Fish are nutritious and often plentiful. There are numerous ways to catch fish, including spearing, trapping, netting, and noodling (which is catching them with your hands) but the average person without prior experience is unlikely to have much luck with these methods. Most people, however, can improvise a fishing pole, hook, and lure.

370 Find Fish

Just before dawn and just after sunset can be good times to catch fish. Fish often shelter under banks and below rocks. Some kinds of fish like weedy areas that provide cover and food. Obstructions, bends, and junctions of streams are often good spots to fish. In cool waters, the fish often prefer shallow, sun-warmed spots. In hotter waters, they may be found deeper.

371 Make a Fishing Pole, Hook, and Lure

If you have your survival kit, with fishhooks and line, all you need is a long stick or branch for the pole. If you don't have line and hook, you can improvise a hook from a piece of wire, a paperclip, or a piece of metal. You can also make a primitive hook called a gorge. Find a small stick of an inch (2.5 cm) or less, and sharpen both ends into hard points. Cut a notch in the middle (around which you will wind your line.) Line can be improvised from clothing threads, wire, dental floss, or even thin strips of bark. Tie one end of the line around the hook and attach the other end to your pole. Hide the hook inside a piece of soft bait (worm, grasshopper or other insect, or even a piece of cloth). Dangle your hook in the water, and wait for a fish to swallow it. When you pull up, the hook will lodge in the fish's throat. Grab the fish, rather than trying to "reel" it in.

Don't Walk in Circles

One of the leading ways people get themselves into survival situations is due to becoming lost or turned around. Research shows that most of us veer to one side on a regular basis, which causes us to walk in circles. Primitive methods do work to give a generalized heading, but only a good quality magnetic or digital compass and/ or a handheld GPS unit can give you real direction finding accuracy. While there are certainly survival situations in which trusting your instincts is a reasonable way to go, being lost is not among them. Don't walk in circles. Find a safe spot and stay there. Use your mind and your instincts to help figure out where you are rather than heading off in what seems like a good direction.

Learn How to Use a Compass

A compass is an essential piece of equipment for any hiker or camper. Unlike GPS, a compass requires no satellite signal and no power sources. What you can do with a compass:

- Find out the direction you are traveling in, i.e., your heading
- Discover the direction of where you want to go, i.e., the bearing
- Travel in a straight line
- Align your map with the actual land
- Figure out your location with a map, or "triangulate"
- Plan your route

Take an Accurate Compass Reading

A compass needle points to the nearest magnetic field. In the northern hemisphere, a compass points north; in the southern hemisphere, the compass needle points south. Adjust your compass for magnetic declination, or the difference between magnetic north and true north. Visit these sites to find out how: www.ngdc.noaa.gov or http://geomag.nrcan.gc.ca/calc/mdcal-en.php

- Hold your compass in front of you, about waist high.
- Be sure to hold a compass level and steady. The needle should swing freely.
- When taking a bearing, do not move your head; lift and lower your eyes. Always use the same eye.
- Turn your whole body until you are directly facing the object you are measuring.
- To prevent an incorrect reading caused by magnetic interference, do not take readings near objects made of metal, even small ones. Don't rest the compass on the hood of your car, for example.
- Take bearings twice.
- When walking a bearing make sure to follow the direction of travel arrow, not the compass needle!

375 Find Magnetic North

Set the compass dial or housing at zero degrees in relation to the direction of travel arrow. Holding the compass in front of you, turn your body until the "red is in the shed," i.e., the magnetic needle is fully in the orienting arrow. Now you are facing magnetic north.

376 Use a Compass to Get Your Bearing

If you have no map, but can see a landmark, you can find a bearing for your destination. Face your landmark, turn the dial until the orienting arrow and the magnetic arrow are lined up. The angle at the top of the compass that is aligned with the direction of travel arrow is your bearing.

377 Take a Back Bearing

You get a back bearing by adding or subtracting 180 degrees from your original bearing.

378 Use a Compass and Map Together

- Place your topographical map on a flat, metal-free surface and put your compass on top of it.
- Draw a line from your starting point (A) to your

destination point (B).

- Line up the edge of the compass baseplate with the A to B line, making sure that the direction of travel arrow is pointing towards B from A.
- Rotate the housing until the red is in the shed. The direction of travel arrow will now be pointing towards your destination.

Carry the Right Maps

379

It is foolish to go on any kind of trip without the right maps. Make sure to carry appropriate topographical maps and/or nautical charts, based on the activities you are planning. Detailed, large-scale topographical maps are essential because they show important land and water details, plus human infrastructure such as buildings, roads, railroads, and hydro lines. Nautical charts show you what's below the water, as well as important safety markings. Maps also show you coordinates, such as the latitude and longitude and Universal Transverse Mercator (UTM) systems. Using maps regularly will help you get to know the map symbols and scale of what things on a map look like in the real world, an invaluable skill when out in the wilds.

Find Your Coordinates

380

Latitude and longitude coordinates are used internationally by most SAR units. Lines of latitude and longitude are measured in degrees, which are divided into minutes and seconds. Latitude increases north or south from the equator, and longitude increases west or east from the zero line or Prime Meridian (at Greenwich, England). Latitude is always given before longitude (49° N 100° E) Degrees West and South are sometimes referred to as negative degrees (-12° -23° is the same as 12 S 23 W)

Bring a GPS Unit

381

Global Positioning System or GPS receivers are highly useful tools for those who venture into the outdoors. They can provide information on your current location, directions to your destination, and track your progress from A to B. There are a variety of excellent, dependable handheld GPS units on the market. Find one that is not a glutton for power. If you can, ask park rangers for recommendations on models or manufacturers.

382 Try Mapping Software

Today you can easily find mapping software that is less expensive than full-sized maps and very convenient, including topographical maps, nautical charts, hiking trails, and even snowmobile and offroading trails. In many cases, these are compatible with some of the GPS models.

383 Don't Use Cell Phones for Mapping

In an emergency situation, a smart phone can be used as a digital compass, GPS unit, or source of topographical mapping (with available apps). However, I suggest you refrain from these uses unless absolutely necessary, since the most important use of the unit is to make emergency calls or texts (and secondarily, to obtain current weather reports and warnings). Save your power for when you need it.

384 Find North Using an Analog Wristwatch

If you have an analog watch (that is, one with hands and dial), you can use it to get your bearings.

- Aim the hour hand (the small hand) at the sun.
- The halfway point between the hour hand pointed at the sun and twelve noon on the dial is a north-south axis (pointing south in the northern hemisphere, and north if you are in the Southern hemisphere).

385 Find Direction with a Shadow Stick Sundial

- On a patch of dirt or sand, jab a straight stick at least 2 feet (60 cm) long into the ground.
- Use a smaller twig or stone to mark the end of the

resulting shadow.
- Wait at least 15 minutes.
- Mark the new shadow with another stone or twig.
- Draw a line from the shadow #1 to shadow #2 — this is a west-to-east line (since the sun travels from east to west, the shadow must go opposite!)

This method works best in open areas, rather than in forested regions where you have to repeat frequently.

Find North at Night

On a clear night in the northern hemisphere, if you can see the constellation known as the Big Dipper (Ursa Major), you can find Polaris, or the North Star. Polaris lies almost due north, and does not rise or set, but stays pretty much in the same location all the time. Looking at the Big Dipper, find the star at the end of the cup. From there, look upwards to find the Little Dipper. The star at the end of the Little Dipper's handle is the North Star.

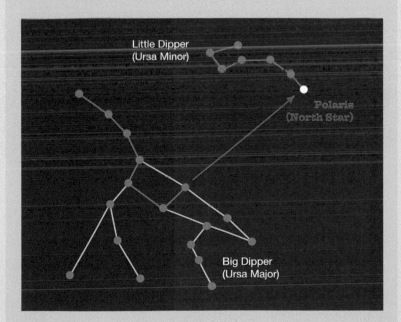

Little Dipper
(Ursa Minor)

Polaris
(North Star)

Big Dipper
(Ursa Major)

387 Improvise Insect Repellant

If you've lost your emergency supplies while in woods or jungle, you may need to improvise a way to repel bugs.

- Smoky fires from burning rotted or green wood and tree fungus are effective at repelling insects.
- Mud applied to the skin works amazingly at both preventing and soothing insect bites.
- Covering up with evergreen boughs may deter blackflies and deer flies, though not mosquitoes.

388 Deter Mosquitoes with a Smoke Pot

Take any tin can, poke some holes around the sides, place some red coals inside and punky wood on top. Place these small smoke smudge pots around your camp site.

389 Keep a Clean Campsite

Deter dangerous wildlife from coming around your camp:

- Never set up tents next to campfire or cooking area
- Never keep any food, drinks, or strong-smelling items in your tents! Hang them (see tip # xx)
- Scrape all food particles into garbage before washing.
- Dump out dishwater at least 100 yards (91 m) from your campsite
- Wash hands after cooking or handling food, and do not sleep in the clothes you wore to cook

390 Hang Food in Trees

To keep your food safe from bears and other wildlife, hang it:

- a minimum of 12 feet (3.6 m) high off the ground, and
- 10 feet (3 m) from the tree trunk, and
- 5 feet (1.5 m) down from the branch it's hanging from.

Treat garbage the same way; pack it out. Alternatively, use approved bear-proof containers.

Deter Bears

Although bears do not usually attack humans, bears are extremely dangerous. One hard swipe or bite can kill. A bear that is habituated to humans may be deadly. When traveling in bear country, take the following precautions:

- Make a lot of noise. Talk, sing, and clap your hands, especially when traveling upwind, rounding a bend or corner, or approaching a stream or waterfall. (So-called "bear bells" may not be loud enough.)
- Watch for signs such as scat (dark, round patties), overturned rocks or moss patches (bears look beneath them for grubs), claw marks on trees, ripped up logs, and devoured berry patches.
- Bears are most active at dawn, dusk, and nighttime— do not travel at night, and be especially alert during these times.
- Keep children close to you at all times.
- Do not travel alone; if you hike or jog down trails by yourself, or camp out solo, you present a better target for a predator.
- Do not bring pets along.
- Never approach a bear cub.
- Set off bear bangers to deter approaching bears from coming closer.
- If you surprise a bear or one surprises you, do not run away. Back away slowly, making noise, trying to look larger than you are, and avoiding eye contact.
- Leave the bear an escape route.

Keep Your Bear Spray Close

A canister of bear spray at the bottom of your pack is not going to help you. If you are in bear country, keep it holstered on your belt. Practice with a spare can before you go so that you will know how to use it:

- Do not spray into the wind—it will blow the chemical back on you.
- Pull back the safety and spray at the spot the bear is coming toward.

- The spray will create a wall of chemical irritant, giving you a chance to move away to safety.

393 Survive a Close Bear Encounter

When trekking through known bear country, you should be armed with bear spray and bangers. Bangers are like flares. They are fired into the air—not at the bear—making a loud noise to scare the bear away. However, if the bear refuses to leave and obviously intends you harm, prepare to fight back. You cannot outrun or outclimb a bear.

- If you're with others, work as a group.
- Shine a flashlight into the bear's eyes to blind it.
- Try to put something solid—a tree or large rock—in between you and the bear, while you search for a weapon such as a large branch or your bear spray or banger.
- Use any weapon you have—throw sticks and stones, your backpack, or whatever you can find at the bear; hit it with a branch or heavy flashlight. Direct your attack toward the bear's snout and eyes.
- If you can, move uphill, striking at the bear as you try to move away (not running).
- Protect smaller members of your party.

394 Watch for Cougars and Moose

Cougars, or mountain lions, are common in many wooded areas, and may be predatory. Moose, though not predatory, are irritable and may charge. Give them a wide berth. For the most part, following the advice for dealing with bears will keep you safe from other large animals.

395 Avoid Snakes

In snake country, wear high-ankle (or higher) hiking boots, thick socks, and thick pants.

- Never reach hands or feet into places you haven't checked
- Use a flashlight so you can see the ground at night

Assess the Ice

"Thick and blue, tried and true; white and crispy, way too risky." Clear, transparent new ice, which may look blue or black, is the safest kind, strong and stable; opaque white, or snow ice, is less thick, more unstable, and less safe. River ice tends to be weaker than lake ice. Avoid iced-over running water, strong currents, and swamps.

Practice Ice Safety

- Wear a PFD during any ice activity
- Never go out on the ice alone or at night
- More than one person? Spread out; walk in single file.
- Bring a pole, ice pick, and measuring equipment
- Bring an ice emergency kit (firestarter, whistle, rope, blanket)

Measure Ice Thickness

When venturing out on frozen bodies of water such as ponds, lakes, or rivers, measure the ice's thickness using an ice auger, chisel, or drill to push through the ice to the water below, and then a tape measure to take the measurement. Follow these rules for new, clear ice only:

- 3 inches (7.5 cm) or less: **Stay off**
- 4 inches (10 cm): Safe for activities on foot such as snowshoeing or skiing, ice fishing
- 7 inches (17.5 cm) Okay for snowmobile or ATV
- 8 to 12 inches (20 to 30 cm) Safe for car or small pickup truck
- 12 to 15 inches (30 to 37.5 cm): Medium truck

For snow ice, double these numbers.

Get Out of Icy Waters

If you fall through the ice, you have little time before hypothermia sets in—you must get out , dry, and warm fast.

- Keep hands and arms on the ice and tread water.
- With hands and arms on the ice, kick your feet to bring your body into a horizontal position.
- While kicking, start to pull with your hands to draw your body onto the ice.
- Roll, crawl, and slide across the ice to safety, keeping your weight spread out.

400 Save Someone Who Falls Through the Ice

Call 911. **Preach, reach, throw, row, go:**

- Call out to the victim to reassure and calm them.
- Extend a rope, ladder, or stout pole to the victim. Let go if you are in danger of being pulled in.
- Throw a rope, PFD, or buoyant object to the victim. Ask the person to tie the rope around their waist.
- If you can, push a boat across the ice to the hole, then get in and pull the victim out.
- Go get the victim by lying down and inching across the ice; if there are several people, create a human chain with each rescuer lying on the ice, holding the feet of the one in front.
- Once out, treat for hypothermia (see tip # xx).

401 Boat Safely

Before going boating, take a boat safety course. Never:

- Boat under the influence
- Operate a boat recklessly or aggressively
- Boat without checking the weather first
- Overload a boat with more weight/people than recommended

Always:

- Make sure every person in a boat is wearing a PFD
- Go out in a properly maintained craft only
- Try to always have 3 points of contact with the boat
- If you are driving, wear an engine cut-off lanyard

- If water is below 50°F (10°C), stay close to shore
- Bring a boating emergency kit

Assemble a Boating Emergency Kit 402

- PFDs for all
- First aid kit
- Fire extinguisher
- Whistle
- 2-way radio
- paddles/oars
- bailer
- anchor
- sun protection
- drinking water

Rescue a Person Overboard 403

- Shout "man overboard." Keep eyes on the victim. Point at the victim.
- Throw a flotation device or looped rope to the victim.
- If the vessel cannot stop, keep throwing buoyant things toward the victim to create a trail.
- Ask victim to loop rope around self: use it to pull victim into boat, keeping victim's back to the rescuer.

Avoid Cold Shock 404

In water that is near freezing, if you fall in, your first response is to gasp for air (gasp reflex action). If you know you are going in, try to cover your face/mouth with your hands to prevent this cold shock and gasp reflex.

Survive Falling Overboard 405

If you are wearing your PFD, the main danger is cold. Pull your knees to your chest and hold them, to help conserve body heat. In warmer waters, tread water or do the dead man's float until you are rescued.

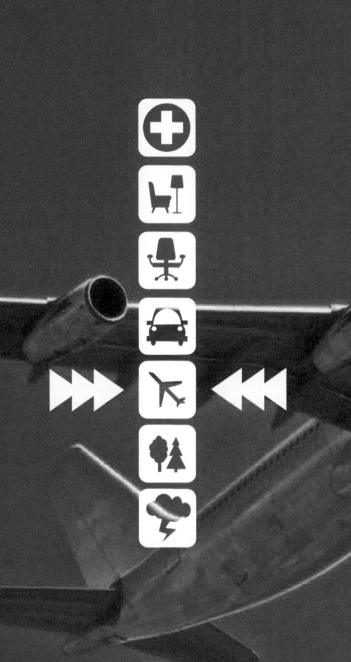

SURVIVE TRAVELING

SURVIVE TRAVELING

> " *Be prepared,*
> *not scared.*"
> —Peter Kummerfeldt

Today's world is tremendously accessible, with even the highest mountains, densest forests, and remotest polar landscapes just a few flights away. Just because you can go almost anywhere, however, doesn't mean that you should! When you do go, and whether it is a vacation, business trip, or holiday gathering—it's essential to take time to properly plan your itinerary, pack appropriately. Your survival mindset means that you also take some extra time to consider what could go wrong, and then make extra preparations so that you'll be ready for it. Foreign countries can pose challenges ranging from illness to theft and worse; research your destination and know both the dangers and sources of help before you get there. Even trips closer to home can land you in difficulty, whether it's dangerous weather or getting lost, so why not be ready?

Know Before You Go

406

Before you plan travel to any foreign country, first check with your own country's consulate or government agency in charge of travel to determine if there are any travel advisories or warnings. The United States Department of State issues short-term Travel Alerts for countries in which situations have arisen that could pose a danger, such a flu outbreak, dangerous weather pattern, or a political disruption; they issue the much stronger Travel Warning for countries that they consider actively risky for such reasons as civil war or terrorist activity. The Canadian government's Travel Advice and Advisories assigns every country one of four possible risk levels, from "No significant security concerns" to "Avoid all travel." Be smart and change your plans if there are Warnings or Advisories for your destination; if you must go there, plan your safety net carefully.

407 Register with Your Own Country

If you are traveling to a foreign country, make a note of the nearest consulate or embassy of your home nation, so you can contact them easily. Register when you arrive.

408 Do Not Travel to Unsafe Places

Do not visit war zones, places where terrorism is common, disorderly regions or locales where there is no rule of law or functioning government, places where extreme weather is likely, or anywhere that is experiencing an outbreak of serious illness or violence.

409 Research Your Destination

Take time to learn about the conditions and culture of your proposed destination before you arrive.

410 Use a Travel Agent

An experienced travel agent with expertise in the type of journey you plan to take (whether it's a theme park or a wildlife safari, there is likely a travel agent who specializes in it) will be an excellent source of information about your destination, and can provide you with support from afar.

411 Research Vendors

Past performance is a good indicator of the quality of any business that caters to tourists, from hotels to activity providers such as fishing guides or "swim with the dolphins" outfits. Before you sign up, do your research to gain a good sense of the company or individual's record. Many online travel sites and forums offer detailed reviews.

Get Travel Documents in Advance

At least six weeks before you travel, make sure your passport (and those of anyone traveling with you) is valid and not due to expire soon. Check whether any of your destinations require a visa, and apply for it well in advance. Make two copies of it, file one and keep another copy with your other travel document copies.

Make Copies of Your Documents

Before you go, make two photocopies of all your travel documents. If your documents are lost or stolen, or in case of emergency, you will be covered. Leave one copy with a relative or friend at home. Keep the other copy with you, but in a separate location from the originals. A digital copy on a small flash drive is a compact option.

- Passport (identification page)
- Foreign visa(s) (if needed)
- Full itinerary
- Hotel confirmations
- Airline tickets
- Driver's license
- Credit cards
- Emergency contact/medical information card

Get Travel Health Insurance

Before any foreign travel, particularly if you are bringing family members, get travel health insurance that includes:

- coverage for all medical services needed while abroad
- coverage for any medications
- transport back to your country for medical care
- transport of your body back to your country if you die

If you plan to hike or visit remote territory on your trip, you should add Search and Rescue coverage. There have been examples of people who've been rescued, but then detained until they paid the full cost of their rescue.

415 Update Immunizations

Check which immunizations are recommended for each region you plan to visit. Research common diseases (such as malaria, hepatitis, or dengue fever) you may encounter at your destination. Call your physician well in advance of your departure with a complete list of your destinations, and be sure to obtain the right shots and preventive medications, as well as any necessary medicines.

416 Designate a Contact Person

Choose at least one reliable person to be your emergency contact. Provide that person with a detailed itinerary and make sure they know how to contact you in an emergency.

417 Enable Communication

Bring one or more reliable communications device:

- smart phone—with appropriate service plan
- personal tracking device
- satellite phone

Make sure you have chargers and back-up power packs.

418 Know the Emergency Number

Every country has an emergency number. Find out how to call for help at your destination, and share the number with your travel companions.

419 Assemble a Basic Travel Survival Kit

In addition to appropriate survival-consideration clothing and footwear for the climate and season at your destination, plus specific clothing for specialized adventures, such as wetsuit/ drysuit, hiking boots, etc., bring:

- copies of ID and documents
- emergency contact/medical information card

- personal medications
- prepaid telephone calling card
- small toiletries kit with toilet paper, wipes, soap, hand sanitizer, sunscreen
- first aid kit (include anti-diarrheals, antibiotics)
- dry sack for valuables
- compact water purification supplies (see tip # xx)
- small emergency survival kit (see tip # xx, about mini kit in a small tin with just a few items)

Pack Medications Properly

420

- Always pack medications in your carry-on bag
- Bring a supply sufficient to last the entire trip, plus a week's extra
- Carry all medications in their original labeled containers
- Make a note of the generic name of your medications in case you need to purchase any while abroad
- For extra safety, obtain from your physician a letter describing your medication regimen

Bring Maps

421

Bring maps of your destination, either printed out in advance or stored in your digital device. If you will be hiking or venturing into nature, a compass and handheld GPS would be wise, as well as your wilderness survival kit.

Use Public Transportation Safely

422

If you intend to use public transportation while traveling, research in advance so you know which lines are officially authorized, where they can take you, how much they cost, and when they operate. Understand how and where to pay the fare. Print and bring maps and schedules with you from home (don't rely on being able to download locally).

- Do not board any vehicle that seems unsafe, due to disrepair, crowding, or other factors
- Stay awake, and keep your belongings and bags close, and valuables out of sight and secure
- Stay awake and alert

423 Dress to Travel

Wear comfortable clothing and shoes that are suitable for emergency situations.

424 Fly Right

Start your airplane trip off right by arriving at the airport with plenty of time to spare, and stay alert from the moment you arrive, keeping your baggage close at all times (and properly tagged with identifying information plus a ribbon or other marker you will recognize). Be sure that checked bags are marked for the correct destination.

- Do not put heavy items in the overhead bins (so they don't fall on you)
- Do not check valuables—put them in your carry-on

425 Tuck a Mini Emergency Kit in Your Carry On

Security regulations make packing a survival kit in your carry-on bag somewhat challenging, but it can be done. Into a small pack, put:

- first aid kit with blunt scissors
- water purification tablets
- hand sanitizer
- space blanket
- disposable lighter
- compass
- sunblock
- collapsible water bottle

426 Walk When You Fly

On any flight longer than 2 hours, make sure you get up out of your seat at least once per hour to walk around on the airplane. A long car or train trip

Survival Story

A couple traveling from North America to Asia arrived at their destination safely and on time, but their luggage took several days to reach them. Fortunately, they'd thought ahead and dressed in comfortable, versatile clothing that could be worn for several days. A change of underwear and a clean t-shirt in their carry-on would have been even better.

also requires regular stops to stretch your legs and move around. This will help to prevent Deep Vein Thrombosis, a potentially fatal blood clot that can be caused by long periods of sitting. If you cannot get up and walk around, move around in your seat raising and lowering your legs, pointing and flexing your toes. Before any trips, ask your doctor if you have any risk factors for DVT, and take the following precautions:

- Do not drink alcohol before or during your flight
- Do not take diuretics before or during your flight
- Avoid caffeine while flying
- Stay hydrated
- Ask your doctor about compression hose

Use a Child Safety Harness

Though not mandatory, safety experts unanimously recommend using an approved Child Restraint System on all flights for infants through children weighing up to 44 lbs (20 kg).

Note Your Exit

Make a mental note of the location of emergency exits relative to your seat, so you can find them in case of emergency, and pay attention to the safety briefing.

Confirm the Flotation Device

Feel under your seat to see that the life jacket (usually in a plastic bag) is there.

Stay Alert During Take-off and Landing
430

Accidents, though rare, tend to happen then, so it's best to stay alert.

Keep Your Seatbelt Fastened
431

Turbulence is the main in-flight danger.

432 Do Not Inflate the PFD Inside the Plane

Wait till you are out; if the plane fills with water before you can exit, you need to be able to dive and swim out. An inflated PFD will trap you inside.

433 Brace for Impact

Bracing prevents you from being thrown forward and injured.

- Put your seat in the upright position, and keep your feet under you
- Bend forward and rest your head on your knees or the seat in front of you
- Place your hands behind your head with elbows on either side

434 Jump Out Onto the Slide

If you have to deplane using the slide, cross your arms in front of you and jump. This is when you'll be happy you wore sensible shoes and pants.

435 Don't Lose Your Luggage

Update your luggage tags every time; don't forget backpacks, and place a luggage tag or other identifying information inside your bag as well.

- Label valuable items in your bags with your name and contact info
- Customize your bag with a ribbon, bandana, stickers, or other identifiers
- Take a photo of your bags and make a packing list
- Use a luggage tracking device
- If your luggage is lost, file a report immediately

436 Bring an Abandon Ship Bag

If traveling by water, your survival kit should be packed in a waterproof go-bag that has flotation ability. Inside, pack:

- Personal Locator Beacon
- Flares, whistle, and signal mirror
- Pocket knife or multi-tool
- Sealed emergency water packets
- MREs (ready-to-eat ration packs)
- Space blanket
- Bailer
- Sunscreen
- Solar still
- Fishing line and hook

Cross Pack 437

If traveling with a companion, consider packing some essential items or duplicates of them, plus one change of clothing in the companion's bag, so you will have them even if one person's bags are lost.

Obtain an International Driving Permit 438

If you plan to drive while in another country, be sure to get an International Driving Permit before you go. The American and Canadian Automobile Clubs are authorized to issue these. Carry both your regular driver's license and your IDP.

- Learn and follow the local rules of the road
- Get insurance
- Wear a seatbelt
- Know where you are going
- Do not pick up hitchhikers or strangers
- Confirm a spare tire and emergency equipment
- Never let gas tank go below half-full

Don't Drink the Water 439

Check the quality of the drinking water in advance by researching online. The water in many countries, while fine for locals, can nevertheless sicken tourists. Stick to factory-sealed bottled water wherever possible, and if in doubt of the seal, choose carbonated bottled water. Do not drink tap water and avoid ice cubes. Bring your own system to filter/purify water just in case. (See tip # xx.) Small portable heater coils can be a practical way for travelers to boil small quantities of water. Alternatively, carrying a water bottle along with a small, portable kettle (with electrical outlet and current flexibility), is another inexpensive way to ensure a reliable supply of purified water. If no other choices are available, tap water that is too hot to touch should also be reasonably safe to drink once it has cooled. Properly collected and stored rainwater is usually safe to drink.

440 **Eat Wisely**

Many travelers do not realize that foodborne illness is more common than waterborne disease, and they fail to pay sufficient attention to what they eat, putting them at risk for traveler's diarrhea, bacterial and viral infections, and diseases that can be transmitted through contaminated food. In general, you will be safest with foods that have been well cooked and are served hot.

- Avoid salad bars (lettuce is difficult to clean), raw vegetables, fruits without peels. Fruits and vegetables should be either freshly peeled/washed in clean water (by you) or freshly cooked
- Do not eat raw and incompletely cooked seafood or meat
- Children should not eat large reef fish such as snapper, barracuda, grouper, jack, and moray eel, which carry the risk of ciguatera poisoning
- Do not eat food from street vendors
- Stay away from dairy products (even ice cream) unless they are pasteurized and have been stored in a fridge
- If traveling with a baby, stick with breastmilk or bring premixed formula

> **SURVIVAL TIP**
>
> Even swimming in a polluted water source can be dangerous. Many natural and manmade pollutants are microscopic, so you won't see them. Keep your mouth closed while swimming—and showering.

Wash Your Hands

441

Often, and always before eating. Dry them, too. If you cannot wash, use an alcohol-based hand sanitizer.

Prevent with Pepto

442

Adults may take bismuth subsalicylate (AKA Pepto-Bismol) to prevent traveler's diarrhea. Check with your doctor first to be sure it is safe for you. The recommended dose is 2 tablets 4 times per day, for up to 3 weeks.

Do Not Get Bitten

443

If traveling to a mosquito-plagued area, bring a mosquito net, and a supply of effective insect repellent:

- DEET products with a concentration of 20 to 35% for adults, and less than 10% for children (Do not apply DEET products to the face or under clothing)
- Picaridin 7% products, which are safe for children and pregnant women
- Oil of lemon eucalyptus, only on those older than 3 years
- Permethrin products, which may be used ONLY ON CLOTHING OR NETS, NEVER ON SKIN

Breathe Easy

444

Some cities, such as Beijing, suffer from significant air pollution. If smog is an issue where you are going, bring face shield masks to protect yourself. This is especially important for children, asthmatics, the elderly, and anyone with breathing or health issues. Most countries post smog warnings, and these should be adhered to by taking precautions, such as staying indoors, and wearing a mask if you have to venture out.

Protect Yourself from Criminals

445

Thieves and other criminals often target tourists, deeming them excellent targets for pickpocketing wallets and purses, muggings, room burglaries, abductions for ransom, and scams and other fraudulent activities. Be aware that you may be a target and take precautions:

- Do not venture into obviously unsafe, dark, unpeopled, or otherwise dangerous neighborhoods or areas
- Stick to main roads, well-lit and lively areas. Do not drive off the beaten path or venture into areas of desperation; do not stop on a lonely stretch of road
- Be cautious about trusting strangers, and avoid getting overly familiar with strangers, especially if their offers seem too good be true

446 Do Not Be Flashy

Do not flash money, jewelry, expensive cameras, computer equipment, phones, or make other displays of wealth.

447 Consult Maps Privately

It's best to review your maps before you go out; standing on a street corner poring over a map or obviously following directions on your phone broadcasts your vulnerability.

448 Deter Pickpockets

Thieves may try to distract you or swarm you. Be aware.

- Carry a cross-body bag; hold it in front of you and close to your body
- Keep a hand on your bag when on public transportation or in a crowd
- If you carry a wallet, keep it in your front pocket
- If you must put your bags down, keep a hand or constant eye on them
- Carry only what you need for the day

449 Keep a Backpack Secure

In general, keep a minimum of valuables in your pack. If you must travel with a camera or laptop, consider not bringing your most expensive model.

- Put a lock on it. A small padlocks or combination lock will deter opportunistic thefts
- Keep valuables (including cash, credit cards, and ID) separately in small bags or pouches on your person
- Use a backpack protector made of mesh
- If you must carry a laptop or tablet, consider getting a laptop lock or a lockable case for the device

Travel Alone Safely

450

If traveling alone, tell other people of your plans and itinerary—every day. Give a copy of your itinerary to at least one person back home, and check in with them regularly. During your trip, be sure let hotel concierge or staff know your plans whenever you leave. If you intend to hike alone, always let someone know your planned route (and stick with it) as well as your expected return time.

Lodge Safely

451

Always keep your door locked. If there is a security chain or latch, fasten it. Avoid ground floor rooms. If window entry is possible, keep windows shut and locked. Don't answer the door if you're not expecting someone or cannot confirm that the person is with your hotel. Consider a travel door alarm.

Separate Identification and Money

452

Keep your passport, cash, and credit cards in 3 separate places to prevent loss of all of it once. Keep just one credit card and the minimum cash needed for the day in your wallet or purse, and put extra money and a back-up card in a separate zippered pouch kept elsewhere on your person, concealed in your luggage, or stashed in the hotel safe.

Use the Safe

453

If your lodging has a safe, use it to store your passport and funds that you do not need with you. If you store cash, put it in a sealed envelope with your name on it and note the amount. Keep a photocopy of your passport's ID page on you when you are out of the room.

454 Call for a Taxi

Do not hail a cab; call one yourself or have a trusted member of the hotel concierge staff arrange for a car for you.

455 Check the Exits

When you board a vessel or vehicle, stay in a hotel room, visit an attraction, or attend a gathering, take a moment to locate the emergency exit or best way out.

456 Bring a Personal Flotation Device

Ferry rides, tour boat trips, and other tourist jaunts that involve water vary enormously in terms of safety precautions; there may not be enough PFDs for everyone aboard, lifeboats may not be accessible, and panic may prevent people from getting to the equipment in time. If your trip involves any kind of water travel, from a ferry ride to a white-water rafting trip, consider bringing your own, tested, high-quality PFD. In case of a listing or sinking boat, you will be glad you have brought and are wearing your own life jacket.

457 Operate Pleasure Craft with Care

Every passenger must wear a PFD. Before getting on any boat, ensure the vessel is in perfect working order, has the proper lights, is fully fueled, and is equipped with bailers, oars, distress signals, fire extinguisher, working communications, and navigational charts. Do not operate any craft while intoxicated!

Survival Story

When the cruise ship *Costa Concordia* ran aground off the coast of Italy, chaos ensued as the poorly trained crew left passengers to fend for themselves. Some survivors, unable to gain access to overcrowded lifeboats, put on life jackets and were able to swim to safety. Others, unable to find life jackets or access lifeboats, perished.

Escape a Sinking Ship

458

In a sinking ship situation, put on your PFD immediately, then help your companions with theirs. Listen for the evacuation signal: 7 short horn blasts followed by a long one. Follow instructions.

- Get to the outer decks. Inner deck areas are more dangerous
- Head up to get out
- If the ship is listing, try to stay upright, grabbing onto supports as you move
- Get on a lifeboat
- If you cannot get on a lifeboat, grab a flotation device
- Look before you leap or step into the water

Practice Anti-Piracy

459

Research the region and strictly avoid areas of known pirate attacks.

- In port, check with local authorities and boaters
- Be sure your on-board communications equipment is in perfect working order
- Use the Universal Shipborne Automatic Identification System (AIS) and keep it on
- Know how to put out an emergency call
- Report and register your travel plans with official maritime organizations; keep your AIS

Never Rely on Others to Save You

460

Don't rely on foreign tour guides, ship captains, hotel operators, or other authority figures to be prepared in a disaster or to provide lifesaving services. Many countries have few or no safety protocols, nor do they require tour operators to have them. There are many recent examples of tourist disasters, including captains abandoning sinking ships, scuba divers left in shark-infested waters, hikers abandoned overnight, hotels lacking fire extinguishers or sprinklers, and criminal gangs preying on tourists. You are responsible for your own safety; take it seriously.

CHAPTER 6

SURVIVE A DISASTER

SURVIVE A DISASTER

Disasters, though rarer than Hollywood would have you believe, do happen. Natural disasters include extreme weather events such as deadly storms, seismic disruptions such as earthquakes, and even seemingly science-fictional events such as solar flares. Human-sponsored disasters range from war to devastating pollution. Some disasters are easier to prepare for than others; unpredictability and events of great magnitude are usually more problematic. Having made it to this chapter, you already know that preparation and mindset are your best assets. Also, never take an elevator during a disaster

> *There is nothing built by man that nature can't destroy in a flash."*
> —Doug Copp

Enable Alert Systems

461

Most governments have set up complex disaster alert systems, using television, radio, cell phone networks, weather networks, and social media. Make sure that you are set up to receive disaster alerts though your smart phone or computing device so that your device beeps or flashes whenever a warning is activated. Immediately get information from an official source and follow authorities' recommendations.

Comprehend Earthquake Danger

462

The major dangers in an earthquake are not from the ground shaking but from falling objects and debris, building collapse, shattered glass, downed power lines, explosions and fires, rockslides and landslides, tsunamis and floods. In less developed places, buildings are often not structurally sound and infrastructure may be crumbling, creating greater danger.

463 Prepare for an Earthquake

If you live in an earthquake zone, where a seismic event rating 7 or higher on the Richter scale can occur, you should regularly practice earthquake drills with your family or household members, and be sure to keep a fully prepped home emergency kit and bug-out bag. Make sure every member of your household knows the family emergency protocols. Hire an inspector to determine whether your home meets earthquake building codes with reinforced supports and beams; bring it up to code and consider extra stabilizing measures. Get earthquake insurance.

464 Quake-proof Your Home

- Keep a 72-hour home survival kit ready (see tip # xx)
- Label on-off positions for water, electricity, and gas and show every member of the household how to turn off water and electricity
- Securely attach to the wall any items that could fall and cause injury: all major appliances, bookshelves, heavy electronics and furniture, mirrors, light fixtures, and other hanging objects
- Move beds away from windows and chimneys, and do not hang shelves or pictures above beds. Close curtains and blinds to prevent shattered glass from falling inward
- Keep a pair of shoes under the bed so you can avoid walking on broken glass
- Secure computers and small appliances with Velcro or rubber grips

- Secure cupboard doors with latches
- Store household chemicals to be unspillable, and keep flammable items away from heat
- Secure water heaters to wall studs or masonry

Indoors: Drop, Cover, and Hold On

465

Most experts recommend that as soon as you feel the shaking, **drop, cover and hold on. Do not run outside. Do not shelter in a doorway. Stay away from windows and exterior walls.**

- Get down on hands and knees
- Protect your head and neck with your hands or a pillow
- Keeping your head covered as you move, take cover beneath a heavy table or desk
- Hold onto the furniture till the shaking stops

Try the Triangle of Life

466

Try the "triangle of life" if you cannot find a sturdy piece of furniture to get under or are in a developing nation. Lie down in a fetal position not under but next to a strong piece of furniture or interior wall, and protect your head and neck with your arms and hands or a pillow. The theory is that, should roofs and walls collapse, crushing furniture, you will be safer in the "buffer space" next to furniture than beneath it.

> ### SURVIVAL TIP
> Leave the wheels on a mobile home or install a structural bracing system to reduce the chance of the house falling off its supports

Stay in Bed

467

If you are in bed when you feel the shaking, stay there, and protect your head with a pillow.

Lock Your Wheels

468

If you use a wheelchair or other mobility device, lock the wheels and remain seated until the shaking stops. Protect your head and neck with your arms, a pillow, a tray, or whatever is available.

469 Stay Outdoors

If you are outside when the earthquake starts, swiftly move away from buildings, streetlights, and electrical wires toward an open area, then drop, cover, and hold on. Stay there until the shaking stops. If you are in a densely built city, quickly run inside a building to avoid falling debris, then drop, cover, and hold on.

Survival Story

Trapped in the rubble of his collapsed hotel in Haiti for 65 hours, a survivor stayed calm, and used his cellphone and a pre-loaded first-aid app to treat his own broken leg and lacerated head. He also set the phone's alarm to go off every 20 minutes so he wouldn't fall asleep, until being found by a French rescue team.

470 Stay in Your Car

Stop in an open space away from buildings, trees, overpasses, and wires

471 Survive if You Are Trapped

- Do not move unduly in order to avoid creating more dust. If you have a cell phone with you, use it to call or text for help
- If you have a whistle, use it; if not, try to make noise by tapping on a wall or other item, so that rescuers can locate you. Avoid yelling unless necessary so you don't lose your voice and inhale dust

472 Survive Post-Quake

- Check for injuries. Provide first aid to anyone who requires help
- Check water, gas, and electric lines; if damaged, shut off the valves
- Check for the smell of gas. If you smell it, open all the windows and doors, leave immediately, and report it to the authorities (use someone else's phone)

- Turn on the radio. Try not to use the phone
- Avoid damaged areas and buildings
- Wear boots or sturdy shoes. Use caution around broken glass and debris
- Implement family emergency communications plan

Understand the Danger of Avalanche 473

Avalanches occur when the snowpack is disturbed and breaks loose, sending massive swathes of snow and ice down the mountain. A full-depth or slab avalanche occurs when the entire snow cover, from earth to surface, breaks loose and rolls down the slope, reaching speeds of 80 mph (130kph) in under 5 seconds. Cornice avalanches occur when overhanging snowpack breaks off and tumbles down the mountain. Any type of avalanche is dangerous.

Weather networks and sites advise regularly regarding avalanche risk, as do local ski patrol units and forest rangers: check the avalanche forecast before you go. Backcountry skiers, snowshoers, hikers, and snowmobilers are at highest risk.

> **SURVIVAL TIP**
> Be prepared to "Drop, cover, and hold on" in the likely event of aftershocks..

Recognize Danger Signs 474

If you will be in avalanche country, take an avalanche education class.

- Convex slopes of 30 to 45 degrees incline are most dangerous
- Avoid barren gullies and slopes with broken trees that may indicate old slide paths or signs of recent avalanche activity
- Smooth slopes are more dangerous than those anchored by rocks and trees
- North-facing slopes are riskier during winter; south-facing slopes are more dangerous in spring, and leeward slopes are more avalanche-prone than windward slopes
- New snow falling rapidly to 1 foot (30 cm) or more and

sustained winds of 15 mph (24 kph) increase the risk
- Warming temperatures or rapid temperature changes

475 Avoid Avalanche

Never:

- Ski or snowmobile out of bounds or off-piste
- Ignore signs posted warning of avalanche zones
- Walk, ski, or snowmobile up to the edge of a drop-off

SURVIVAL TIP

It's a myth that loud noises cause avalanches; it's usually the weight of the person making the noise that causes the instability.

Always:

- Wait at least 48 hours after a big rain or snowstorm
- Bring a transceiver (and keep it on), shovel, and probe with you
- Wear an avalanche air bag or breathing mouthpiece

476 Survive an Avalanche

If you are overtaken by an avalanche, your survival depends on being able to breathe until you are rescued—but chances of survival are extremely slim.

- "Swim" in the direction of the snowslide, trying to stay on top
- Keep your mouth and nose covered; do not scream
- As the slide slows, hold hands in front of your face to create an air pocket
- When you come to a stop, reach a hand toward the surface (if you know where it is)

477 Survive an Ice Storm

Ice storms often come on with little warning. Power lines and tree branches cannot withstand the ice's extra weight, multiple

SURVIVAL TIP

If you have to cross an avalanche-prone slope, do not crisscross but go straight up or down. The safest route is across the top of a ridge. .

lines are often downed, and widespread power outages occur. The biggest danger is from downed electrical lines, which are live and extremely deadly.

- If an electrical line has fallen on your house, evacuate
- If it is safe to do so, move your car where trees or branches can't fall on it
- Do not drive
- Stay in the house
- Do not walk under any trees or hydro lines
- Do not touch or walk over any downed hydro lines
- Utilize sand and deicing compounds for your walkways and adjacent sidewalks

SURVIVAL FACTOID

The great blackout of Eastern North America in 2003 that left at least 50 million people without power was caused by inadequate tree trimming. Electrical lines came into contact with the untrimmed tree branches, and shorted the system, resulting in a systemic cascading grid-to-grid shutdown.

Stay Safe in a Windstorm

478

Fierce windstorms have become increasingly common. Dangers typically come from falling branches, flying debris, downed trees and power lines, and even building collapses. The safest place to be during high winds is indoors. Postpone outdoor activities if a wind advisory or high wind warning has been issued. If you are stuck outdoors during a windstorm:

- Watch for flying debris
- Take cover next to a building
- Stay well back from busy streets, roadways, and train tracks, as a gust may blow you into the path of an oncoming vehicle
- Hold handrails where available.
- Avoid elevated areas such as roofs without adequate railing

Drive Safely in High Winds

479

- Keep both hands on the wheel and slow down
- Do not drive close to other cars in adjacent lanes in

case of strong gusts pushing cars out of their lanes

- High-profile vehicles such as trucks, vans, and SUVs are more prone to be pushed or even flipped by high wind gusts
- If winds are severe enough to prevent safe driving, get onto the shoulder of the road and stop, making sure you are away from trees or other tall objects that could fall onto your vehicle. Stay in the car and turn on the hazard lights until the wind subsides

480 Practice Power Line Safety

Stay away from downed power lines and teach children to give them a wide berth.

- Never touch anything that may be touching a downed power line, including vehicles or tree branches. Puddles and snowy ground have been known to conduct electricity
- Never touch anyone who has been shocked or who may be in direct or indirect contact with a power line. Get the medical attention immediately
- If a power line falls on your car, stay inside. Call 911
- Do not touch the metal frame of your vehicle. Honk your horn, roll down the window, and warn passersby of the danger. Ask someone to call the police. Do not exit the car until help arrives, unless it catches on fire. To exit, open the door, and jump out, without touching any of the metal portions of the car's exterior

> **SURVIVAL FACTOID**
>
> The Beaufort Wind Scale
> 25 - 31 mph (39 – 49 kph): Strong Breeze
> 32 - 38 mph (50 – 61 kph): Moderate Gale
> 39 - 46 mph (62 - 74 kph): Fresh Gale
> 47 - 54 mph (75 – 88 kph): Strong Gale
> 55 - 63 mph (89 – 102 kph): Storm
> 73 + mph: (118 + kph): Hurricane.

481 Prepare for High Winds

Prep your property to lower the risk of damage or injury:

- Remove any dead trees or overhanging branches near structures
- Fix loose roofing materials
- Secure or bring inside any loose items in yards, patios, or on balconies that could blow away, including lawn furniture, bird feeders, or garbage cans

Know Your Windstorm Terminology

482

- **A tropical cyclone** is any circulating weather system that generally forms in the tropics. In the northern hemisphere, winds circulate in a counterclockwise direction; in the southern hemisphere, they circulate clockwise. Tropical cyclones are categorized as follows:
- **Tropical Depression:** An organized system of clouds and thunderstorms with a defined circulation and maximum winds of 38 mph (33 knots) or less
- **Tropical Storm:** An organized system of strong thunderstorms with a defined circulation and maximum sustained winds of 39 to 73 mph (34-63 knots)
- **Hurricane:** An intense tropical weather system with a well-defined circulation and maximum sustained winds of 74 mph (64 knots) or higher
- **Typhoon:** A hurricane in the western Pacific
- **Cyclone:** A hurricane in the Indian Ocean

Prepare for a Hurricane

483

A hurricane "watch" means there is a threat of hurricane conditions within 48 hours. Prepare your bug-out kit. A hurricane "warning" indicates imminent hurricane conditions—within 24 hours. Keep track of the situation via radio, television, and internet. Evacuate immediately if authorities recommend doing so. Otherwise:

- Secure your property by putting up storm shutters or boarding up windows with □-inch (16 mm) marine plywood, cut to fit and ready to install
- If you have a boat, moor it securely
- Use straps or clips to securely fasten your roof to the house frame to help lessen roof damage

- Trim trees and shrubs around your home
- Clear loose and clogged rain gutters and downspouts
- Elevate items stored in your basement
- Bring any loose items from outside your home indoors
- Check and update your 72-hour Home Emergency Kit

484 Know When to Evacuate

Evacuate under the following conditions:

- If you are directed by local authorities to do so
- If you live in a mobile home or temporary structure
- If you live in a high-rise
- If you live on the coast, on a floodplain, near a river, or on an inland waterway
- If you feel that you are in danger

485 Survive a Hurricane

- Turn off utilities if instructed to do so
- Turn refrigerator thermostat to its coldest setting and keep its doors closed
- Turn off propane tanks
- Stay indoors, away from windows and glass doors
- Avoid using the phone, except for serious emergencies
- Ensure a supply of water by filling the bathtub and other large containers with water
- Close interior doors—secure and brace external doors
- Keep curtains and blinds closed
- Take refuge in a small interior room, closet, or hallway on the lowest level

486 Beware a Tornado

A tornado is a violently rotating, funnel-shaped column of cloud that reaches from the base of a thunderstorm down to the ground. A tornado is amongst the deadliest of natural weather events, able to tear apart homes, uproot trees, and hurl vehicles into the air, creating a trail of damage more than a mile (1.6 km) wide and 50 miles (80 km) in length. Tornadoes can strike anywhere, anytime, though they often occur in regions with flat, dry terrain. Tornado Alley is a region of the central United States across northern Texas, Oklahoma, Kansas, and Nebraska where tornadoes occur frequently. In Canada, the prairies and southwestern Ontario see more tornadoes.

Know the Signs of an Impending Tornado

487

Tornadoes can occur with little warning. Take shelter immediately if you see an approaching storm with:

- Dark sky, often with a green tinge
- Large hailstones
- A big, dark, low-lying cloud that may be rotating
- A loud roaring noise

If you see an approaching storm with any of these characteristics, take shelter immediately.

Prepare for a Tornado

488

A tornado "watch" means that tornado conditions are expected; be prepared. In case of a watch, secure your home as in tip # xx<earthquake>. A tornado "warning" means take cover immediately! Close your windows. Take shelter in a customized safe room built specifically to withstand a tornado, a basement shelter/storm cellar, or an interior room on the lowest floor with no windows. A mobile home is not safe. Practice tornado drills with family members. If you have children, check with their schools regarding tornado procedures.

Survive a Tornado Indoors

489

Go to the pre-determined safe room, basement, or interior room on lowest possible floor of the building, such as a hallway or even a closet. Put as many walls between you and the tornado as you can. Get under a sturdy piece of furniture and protect your head. Stay away from windows, and be sure to keep them closed, as high winds and dangerous debris can enter if they're opened.

490 Survive a Tornado Outdoors

If you are caught outdoors, find the lowest spot you can, such as ditch or depression in the ground, then lie flat and cover your head. Be aware of the potential for flash floods. Watch for flying debris, the source of most fatalities during tornadoes. If you are in a car, or can get into one, and can drive, don't try to outrun the tornado; instead drive at a 90-degree angle away from the storm and get to a shelter. If there is too much flying debris, park, keep your seatbelt on, get lower than the window level, and cover your head. Do not seek shelter under a highway overpass.

491 Recover from a Tornado

Follow the instructions in tip # xx <after a flood.>

492 Prepare for Flooding

Many regions on our planet are prone to regular flooding, especially low lying coastal areas, floodplains, and river delta regions, and tropical and humid regions that experience monsoons. Even in more arid regions, flash floods can happen, sometimes hours or days after a rainstorm. Awareness and preparation are crucial to surviving a flood. Practice evacuation of your home with your family. Have a go-bag ready. See tips # xx through xx for specific flood preparations and survival advice.

493 Learn the Risk of Wildfire

Dry regions are prone to wildfires, which are unplanned and uncontrolled fires typically occurring in forest or grasslands. Though some wildfires are started by natural causes—either lightning strikes or lava—most are caused by human error or carelessness, including tossed cigarettes, campfires improperly extinguished, and arson. Wildfires move with speed and ferocity, consuming entire communities, destroying trailer parks and campgrounds, and even engulfing fleeing residents. Check risk levels with the National Fire Danger Rating System in the United States or the Canadian Wildland Fire Information System.

Prepare for Wildfire

494

In addition to following the fire safety and prevention tips in Chapter 2: Survive at Home, take these steps to create a defendable area for at least 30 feet (9 m) around your home:

- Remove all fuels, such as logs, brush, or debris from around your home
- Space trees at least 10 feet (3 m) apart
- Prune branches to at least 6 feet (2 m) above the ground
- Cut back shrubs to no higher than 18 inches (1.5 m)
- Remove dead or dying trees and shrubs
- Keep lawn short and well maintained
- Keep your roof, gutters, and eaves clear of debris
- Never allow tree branches to hang over your roof
- Store firewood and fuel 50 feet (15 m) from the house
- Clear a 10-foot (2m) area around firewood and storage
- Do not connect wooden fencing directly to your home
- Use non-combustible roof and vent screening materials
- Cover exterior walls with fire resistant materials like stucco, stone, or brick
- Use double-paned or tempered glass for exterior windows
- Install non-combustible street signage
- Make sure your address can be seen from the street

Survive a Wildfire

495

If a wildfire has been reported in your area, or worse, it is approaching your home, take the following steps, if you can safely do so, before evacuating:

- Close all windows and doors
- Cover vents, windows, and other openings of the house with duct tape and/or precut pieces of plywood
- Pack your car with a go-bag, and position it facing forward out of the driveway
- Turn off propane or natural gas
- Turn on the lights in the house, porch, garage and yard
- Move combustible materials such as furniture away from the windows
- Place a ladder to the roof in the front of the house
- Put lawn sprinklers on the roof of the house and turn on the water, or hose down the roof
- Move all combustibles away from the house, including firewood, gas bbqs, and lawn furniture

496 Recognize a Landslide

Landslides and mudslides occur when a mound of earth, mud, rocks, and/or debris comes loose and rolls rapidly and violently downhill. Slides occur widely in mountainous or even hilly areas, and may be triggered by heavy rainfall, seismic activity, or poor land use.

Don't build on steep hills, mountain edges, drainage routes, or other potentially unstable ground. Before building, get a professional land assessment.

Do Not Ignore Slide Warning Signs. Any of the following should be cause for concern:

- Visible changes to drainage patterns
- Small slides, flows, or progressively leaning trees
- New or widening cracks in paved areas, foundations, or walls
- Building shifts; walls pulling away
- Tilting fences, retaining walls, utility poles, or trees

If you live a slide-prone area, heavy rainfall or snowmelt should prompt you to pay attention to weather reports and alerts. Many slide victims are caught sleeping. Evacuate if there are signs of imminent landslide or mudslide.

Survive a Landslide

If you are outdoors and see the land begin to shift or feel movement beneath you, immediately:

- Run sideways away from the flow of debris—do not try to outrun it
- Curl into a ball and protect your head

Indoors, move to an interior room on a high floor. When it is over, call for assistance.

Survive a Volcano

A volcanic eruption occurs when the pressure of gases under the earth becomes strong enough to push molten lava up through the top of a mountain. Lava, poisonous gases, flying rocks and debris, superheated air, and waves of airborne ash result. If you live near an active or potentially active volcano, subscribe to your governmental alert system and take all warnings seriously. Evacuate immediately when directed to do so. Higher ground is safer ground. If you are on the mountain or in the "death zone" when an eruption occurs, try to get to higher ground and away from the flow.

- Avoid valleys and low-lying areas that lead away from the mountain
- Move upward to high ground off the valley floor
- Seek shelter and minimize your exposure to ash
- Close non-essential doors, windows, and vents; seal with duct tape
- Place damp towels at the bottom of external doors
- Stay off fresh lava flows
- Do not drive in ashfall
- Do not return to your home or go outside until authorities allow it
- Use an N-95 respirator mask to minimize ash inhalation
- Wear long pants and sleeves, plus goggles
- Follow official instructions for clean-up

499 Live Through a Pandemic

In a pandemic situation, take the following precautions:

- Avoid contact with people who are sick
- If you show symptoms, quarantine yourself
- Cover your mouth and nose if you sneeze or cough
- Wash your hands frequently and use alcohol-based hand sanitizer in between washings
- Avoid touching your eyes, nose or mouth
- Wear a mask or respirator to minimize exposure
- Wear a Tyvek protection suit with hood

500 Be Prepared for an Explosion

Though rare, explosions do occur, typically due to fires, improper gas and chemical transportation and storage, and bombs. If you live near a propane storage facility, a chemical plant, or any other potentially explosive place, or even next to a railroad track, develop a household evacuation and bug-out plan, and keep your emergency survival kits ready.

501 Survive an Explosion

If an explosion is about to occur:

- Run away
- Get low—or hit the ground
- Seek shelter under a sturdy object or behind a barrier
- Cover your head and curl up to protect your body
- Face away from the explosion

502 Survive a Riot

Crowds—even those who've gathered for peaceful or entertainment purposes (not to mention Black Friday at certain retailers)—can quickly turn dangerous when panic or anger sets in. Places that are experiencing civil unrest or a failure of law enforcement can swiftly erupt into extreme violence. The safest course is to stay away from public spaces in such circumstances. If you are caught in a panicked crowd or riot situation, immediately locate potential exits, and:

- If you have a child with you, pick them up and hold them in front of you, arms tightly wrapped around them
- Keep your hands in front of your chest to create space
- Don't fight the crowd; move diagonally with the flow, trying to get to the edge
- Don't rush the doors; you may be crushed against an unopened exit or in a constricted doorway
- Avoid walls/fences where you can be trapped/crushed
- If you fall, try to pull yourself up immediately even if you have to "crawl" up the person in front of you

Survive a Gun Attack

503

Stay out of the line of fire. If possible, run, bringing with you as many people as you can. If you cannot run, hide, and try to prevent the shooter from gaining entry:

- In a lockdown situation, barricade the entry with heavy furniture and objects
- Hide on either side of the entrance, not in front of it
- If the shooter enters, attack from behind, aiming for the knees
- Fight as a group, using all potential weapons to distract, blind, and bring down the shooter

Survive a Hostage Situation

504

To survive a hostage situation, stay calm and try to connect:

- Do not fight back or provoke the hostage-takers; follow instructions calmly
- Relate as a fellow human being—ask for medications, speak of family, avoid sensitive topics, act humanely
- Throughout, remain alert, healthy, hopeful, and be ready for rescue

505   Survive a Chemical Attack

Chemical agents are toxic vapors, aerosols, liquids, and solids. Signs of a chemical release include people having difficulty breathing; experiencing eye irritation; losing coordination; becoming nauseated; or having a burning sensation in the nose, throat, and lungs. In case of a chemical attack:

- Make sure your home or office emergency kit is fully stocked and includes duct tape, scissors, plastic sheeting, and respiratory masks
- Move to an interior room without windows or vents
- Close doors and windows
- Turn off all ventilation, including furnaces, air conditioners, vents, and fans
- Seal off doors, windows, and vent with duct tape and plastic sheeting
- If outdoors, move upwind and seek shelter immediately

506   Survive a Biological Attack

Biological agents are bacteria, viruses, and toxins that can kill or incapacitate. A respiratory mask and hazmat suit can protect you but most people don't keep such items on hand. If you are exposed to a biological agent:

- Remove and bag your clothes and personal items
- Follow official instructions for disposal of contaminated items
- Wash with soap and water and put on clean clothes
- Seek medical assistance
- Stay away from others

507   Know the Location of the Closest Fallout Shelter

Prepare for a nuclear event by knowing where to take shelter in advance. Put this information in your family emergency plan.

Survive a Nuclear Plant Meltdown

508

Distance, shielding, and time are the 3 pillars of protection in case of exposure to nuclear radiation and fallout that may be caused by a nuclear reactor malfunction, fire, or meltdown. Most plants have extensive warning systems.

- An underground area such as a home or office building basement offers the best protection
- A floor near the middle of a highrise may be better, depending on what is nearby at that level on which significant fallout particles would collect
- Flat roofs collect fallout particles so the top floor is not a good choice, nor is a floor adjacent to a flat roof
- Heavy, dense materials such as thick walls, concrete, bricks, books and earth make effective shields
- Put distance between you and the fallout particles
- Fallout radiation loses intensity fairly rapidly, posing the greatest threat in the first two weeks, after which it declines to about 1% of its initial radiation level

Survive a Nuclear Blast

509

A nuclear blast is an explosion with intense light and heat, a damaging pressure wave, and widespread radioactive fallout that can contaminate the air, water, and ground surfaces for miles around. A blast shelter protects you from the initial explosion; a fallout shelter protects you from the radioactive particles.

- Take shelter in a blast shelter or below ground
- If outside, lie flat on the ground facedown, covering your head and eyes
- Get to shelter as fast as you can
- Stay in the shelter for at least 3 days, or until authorities direct you to leave

Never Give Up!

510

HOW TO START A FIRE WITH WATER

HOW TO START A FIRE WITH WATER